Outstanding Teaching Cases Grounded in Research

Volume 38 • Issue 1 • Winter 2018

Case Research Journal

Published by the

North American Case Research Association

N A C R A

Editors

Gina Grandy
University of Regina

John J. Lawrence
University of Idaho

Published quarterly by North American Case Research Association, Inc.

Cover design, Lisa Fahey, originables.com.

NACRA membership for individuals is US $50. To join, register and pay online at:
https://www.nacra.net/members/index.php5

POSTMASTER: Please send address corrections to:

North American Case Research Association
Lynn Southard, Assistant Editor
Case Research Journal
7561-A Suffield Road
Stokesdale, NC 27357

Printed in the United States of America

10   9   8   7   6   5   4   3   2   1

ISSN 2328-5095
ISBN: 978-0-9989176-5-8

NACRA Officers 2017–2018

EXECUTIVE COMMITTEE AND BOARD OF DIRECTORS

Co-Presidents
Kathryn Savage
Northern Arizona University
and
Jeffrey P. Shay
Washington & Lee University

Immediate Past President
John Gamble
Texas A&M University - Corpus Christi

President Elect
Chris Cassidy
Sam Houston State University

Vice-President Programs
Javier Silva
IAE Business School, Universidad Austral

Vice-President Programs-Elect
Open

Vice President, Case Marketing
Susan Sieloff
Northeastern University

Vice President, Membership
Brent D. Beal
University of Texas at Tyler

Vice President, Communications
Lisa Eshbach
Ferris State University

Secretary/Treasurer
A. Kay Guess
Samford University

Outgoing Editor, Case Research Journal
John Lawrence
University of Idaho

Incoming Editor, Case Research Journal
Gina Grandy
University of Regina

REPRESENTATIVES OF REGIONAL AND AFFILIATED ORGANIZATIONS

Canada (ASAC)
Eric Dolansky
Brock University

Mexico (ALAC)
Adriana Ramirez Rocha
Tecnológico de Monterrey

Eastern U.S. (CASE)
William Naumes
University of New Hampshire (Retired)

Southeastern U.S. (SECRA)
Susan Peters
Francis Marion University

Southwestern U.S. (SWCRA)
Simon Metcalf
Augusta University

Western U.S. (WCA)
Michael Valdez
Fort Lewis College

Caribbean Case Researchers Association
Paul Golding,
U Technology - Jamaica

Directors at Large
Gina Grandy
University of Regina
Joe Kavanaugh
Sam Houston State University
U. Srinivasa Rangan
Babson College

Advisory Council Chair
William Naumes
University of New Hampshire (Retired)

Case Research Journal Editorial Policy
North American Case Research Association (NACRA)

CASE CONTENT

The *Case Research Journal* (CRJ) publishes outstanding teaching cases drawn from research in real organizations, dealing with important issues in all administration-related disciplines. The CRJ specializes in decision-focused cases based on original primary research – normally interviews with key decision makers in the organization but substantial quotes from legal proceedings and/or congressional testimony are also acceptable. Secondary research (e.g., journalist accounts, high quality website content, etc.) can be used to supplement primary data as needed and appropriate. Exceptional cases that are analytical or descriptive rather than decision-focused will only be considered when a decision focus is not practical and when there is a clear and important gap in the case literature that the case would fill. Cases based entirely on secondary sources will be considered only in unusual circumstances. The Journal also publishes occasional articles concerning case research, case writing or case teaching. Multi-media cases or case supplements will be accepted for review. Contact the journal editor for instructions.

Previously published cases or articles (except those appearing in Proceedings or workshop presentations) are not eligible for consideration. The Journal does not accept fictional works or composite cases synthesized from author experience.

CASE FORMAT

Cases and articles submitted for review should be single- spaced, with 12-point font and 1" margins. Published cases are typically 8-12 pages long (before exhibits), though more concise cases are encouraged and longer cases may be acceptable for complex situations. All cases should be written in the past tense except for quotations that refer to events contemporaneous with the decision focus.

Figures and tables should be embedded in the text and numbered separately. Exhibits should be grouped at the end of the case. Figures, tables, and exhibits should have a number and title as well as a source. Necessary citations of secondary sources (e.g., quotes, data) should be included as endnotes at the end of the case (not at the end of the IM) in APA format. In the IM, necessary citations (e.g., citations of theoretical work from which the analysis draws) should be included using parenthetical author/year embedded in the text (similar to a traditional academic paper) that feeds into a list of references at the end of the IM. Note that the CRJ approaches citations differently in the case and the IM given the differing audiences for which each document is developed (i.e., the case is written for the student while the IM is written for the instructor). In some rare instances, footnotes may be used in the case for short explanations when including these explanations in the body of the text would significantly disrupt the flow of the case, but generally the use of footnotes in the case should be avoided if possible.

The following notice should appear at the bottom of the first page of the manuscript: Review copy for use of the Case Research Journal. Not for reproduction or distribution. Dated (date of submission). Acknowledgements can be included in a first page footnote after the case is accepted for publication, and should mention any prior conference presentation of the case.

It is the author(s)'s responsibility to ensure that they have permission to publish material contained in the case. To verify acceptance of this responsibility, include the following paragraph on a separate page at the beginning of the submission:

In submitting this case to the Case Research Journal for widespread distribution in print and electronic media, I (we) certify that it is original work, based on real events in a real organization. It has not been published and is not under review elsewhere. Copyright holders have given written permission for the use of any material not permitted by the "Fair Use Doctrine." The host organization(s) or individual informant(s) have provided written authorization allowing publication of all information contained in the case that was gathered directly from the organization and/or individual.

INSTRUCTOR'S MANUAL

Cases must be accompanied by a comprehensive *Instructor's Manual* that includes the following elements:

1. **Case Synopsis**: A brief (three-quarters of a page maximum) synopsis of the case.

2. **Intended Courses & Learning Objectives:** Identification of the intended course(s) that the case was written for, including the case's position within the course and the specific learning objectives that the case was designed to achieve. Please also indicate whether the case was developed for an undergraduate or graduate student audience. For more details on learning objectives, see the article titled "Writing Effective Learning Objectives" at the useful articles link.

3. **Research Methods:** A Research Methods section that discloses the research basis for gathering the case information, including any relationship between case authors and the organization, or how access to case data was obtained. Include a description of any disguises imposed and their extent. Authors should disclose the relationship between this case and any other cases or articles published about this organization by these authors without revealing the author's identity during the review process. If the case has been test taught and this has influenced the development of the case, this should be noted. This section should also indicate who in the organization has reviewed the case for content and presentation and has authorized the authors to publish it (note that this last component is not necessary for cases based on congressional or legal testimonies).

4. **Theoretical Linkages:** In this section please provide a brief overview of the theoretical concepts and frameworks that will ground the analysis/discussion of the case situation in theory and research. Please include associated readings or theoretical material that instructors might assign to students or draw on to relate the case to their field or to the course. In developing this section, recognize that business courses are often taught by adjunct faculty who are business professionals who may not be steeped in the theory of the discipline the way an active researcher might be. Develop this section with the intent of helping that type of instructor effectively apply and teach these theories/frameworks.

5. **Suggested Teaching Approaches:** Suggested teaching approaches or a teaching plan, including the expected flow of discussion with an accompanying board plan. Include a description of any role plays, debates, use of audiovisuals or in-class handouts, youtube videos, etc. that might be used to enhance the teaching of the case. Authors are strongly encouraged to classroom test a case before submission so that experience in teaching the case can be discussed in the *IM*. Authors are discouraged from including websites as integral resources for the teaching plan because websites are not static and the content of the website link may change between the writing of the case and an instructor's subsequent use of the case.

6. **Assignment/Discussion Questions:** A set of assignment/discussion questions (typically three to ten depending on discipline) that can be provided to students to organize and guide their preparation of the case. For most cases, either the final or the penultimate question will ask students for their recommendation on the overarching decision facing the decision maker in the case along with their rationale for that recommendation.

7. **Analysis & Responses to Assignment/Discussion Questions:** This section of the IM represents the core of the case analysis. Repeat each assignment/discussion question, and then present a full analysis of that question that demonstrates application of relevant theory to the case. Note that the analysis in this section should go beyond what a good student might present as an 'answer' to the question. Write to the instructor with an eye toward helping him or her understand in detail how the theory applies to the case scenario, how discussion of this particular question might be approached with students, where the limitations in the theory might be relative to the case scenario, and how the analysis contributes to the building of an integrated recommendation regarding the decision the case protagonist must make.

8. **Epilogue:** If appropriate, an epilogue or follow-up information about the decision actually made and the outcomes that were realized as a result of the decision made.

9 **References**: Provide full citations (in APA format) for all references that were cited in the Instructor's Manual.

Review Process

All manuscripts (both the case and the instructor's manual) are double-blind refereed by Editorial Board members and ad hoc reviewers in the appropriate discipline. Most submissions require at least one round of revision before acceptance and it is common for accepted cases to go through two or more rounds of revisions. The target time frame from submission to author feedback for each version is 60 days.

Distribution of Published Cases

The right to reproduce a case in a commercially available textbook, or instructor-created course pack, is reserved to NACRA and the authors, who share copyright for these purposes. After publication, CRJ cases are distributed through NACRA's distribution partners according to non-exclusive contracts. NACRA charges royalty fees for these publication rights and case adoptions in order to fund its operations including publication of the *Case Research Journal*. Royalties paid are split 50/50 between NACRA and member authors.

Manuscript Submission

Submit the case manuscript and Instructor's Manual in one document via the *Case Research Journal* ScholarOne website at **http://mc.manuscriptcentral.com/nacra-crj**. This site provides step by step instructions for uploading your case. You will also be provided the opportunity to upload two case supplements – this is to allow submission of a spreadsheet supplement for the student and for the instructor if needed. No identification of authors or their institutions should appear on either the main case/IM document or on the spreadsheets. All identifying information should be removed from the file properties before submission. If you have audiovisual content to your case, please contact the editor to determine the best way to make this content available to reviewers without revealing the authors' identities.

At least one author must be a member of the North American Case Research Association. Membership dues are included in annual registration for the NACRA conference, or may be paid separately through the main NACRA website.

For questions, contact:
Gina Grandy, Editor
Gina.Grandy@uregina.ca

Adopting *Case Research Journal* Cases
for use in your classes

Faculty members can adopt cases for use in their classrooms and gain access to Instructor's Manual through one of NACRA's distribution partners.

NACRA currently has agreements with the following distributors.

- **Harvard Business School Press** (http://hbsp.harvard.edu/)
- **Ivey Publishing** (https://www.iveycases.com/)
- **The Case Centre** (http://www.thecasecentre.org/educators/)
- **Pearson Collections** (https://www.pearsonhighered.com/collections/educator-features.html)
- **McGraw Hill Create** (http://create.mcgraw-hill.com/createonline/index.html)
- **Study.net** (www.study.net)
- **CCMP [Centrale de Cas et de Médias Pédagogiques]** (http://www.ccmp.fr)

If you want to use one of these distributors, but cannot find the CRJ case you want, contact the NACRA VP Case Marketing to see if we can have it added for you.

Textbook authors can also adopt CRJ cases for inclusion in their textbooks for a modest fixed royalty fee. Please contact the NACRA VP of Case Marketing for more information.

From the Editors

Welcome to Volume 38 Issue 1 of the *Case Research Journal*. This first issue of 2018, and this 'From the Editors' letter, are collaborations between outgoing editor John Lawrence and incoming editor Gina Grandy. Seeing a case through from initial submission to publication is a lengthy process for both authors and editors, and in the interest of continuity for our authors we are attempting to hand off the editorial oversight of as few in-process cases as possible. We began working to transition executive editor responsibilities last fall, and that process of transition will be completed later this spring. All of the cases in this issue were submitted to the journal during John's tenure as editor, although a variety of editors managed the review process for these cases. John managed two of them and Gina managed one of them. In addition, three of the cases published in this issue were originally submitted to the short case special and their reviews were managed by special issue guest editors Charles Mossman and Brent Beal. So at least with respect to this issue, it takes a village to publish a journal (and that's not even counting the 18 reviewers who contributed to these six cases).

The portfolio of cases that appear in this issue is somewhat unique compared to previous issues of the journal and deserves some comment here. First, half of the cases in this issue are in either the accounting or finance area. We were happy to see these three strong accounting and finance cases reach the point of publication. All have clear decision foci and will likely generate significant classroom debate around those decisions, but all also align with the highly quantitative nature of these disciplines and at least two of the three require significant number crunching for students to be in a position to engage in that debate about what to do. We often hear that such quantitative cases have a difficult path to publication in the CRJ because the number crunching will produce the right answer. That isn't always the case, and these cases demonstrate that. If you are curious about this, start with the Arkansas Egg Company case to see how the numbers inform, but don't define the decision.

Second, a couple of the cases have decision points that are further in the past than we typically publish. In general, we strive to publish cases built around a decision that have occurred within the past five years based on the preference that we see in distribution for very current cases. Occasionally we make exceptions to that target timeframe when the case scenario is particularly unique in a way that is likely to significantly enhance student learning and the case satisfies a pressing need in the body of cases within the discipline. The Monmouth Rubber and Plastics case is a good example. This case is set in the fall of 2008 as the economy is sliding deeper into recession. The owner of this family business has received a quite attractive offer for the business, and the business is facing the added risk that it may be forced out of its current facility as a result of a community redevelopment project and the process of eminent domain. It is in this context that the owners' son, the company's sales manager, makes clear that he would someday in the not too distant future like to take over the business. These, and other components of this case, make it an incredibly rich context to discuss generational transitions in family businesses. Given this unique case setup, we sent it out to reviewers despite its datedness, and the reviewers confirmed that the case would be of significant value in a family business class (although reviewers also made many suggestions that helped shape the case that you see in the journal).

Third, you will notice that one of the cases in the journal, "La Campaña de Marketing de Oilcorp: Reacciones Mixtas a una Iniciativa de Responsabilidad Social," is in Spanish. This case is the Spanish translation of one of the cases published in Volume 37 Issue 4 under the title Oilcorp's Marketing Campaign: Mixed Reactions to a CSR Initiative. While we don't have the capacity to review cases submitted in Spanish or in other foreign languages, we can work with authors from Spanish and French speaking countries to place a Spanish or French translation of an accepted CRJ case into distribution so that these cases can be more broadly adopted within the countries in which the cases are set. The

Oilcorp case went through the traditional CRJ review process in English. But its author, Juan Manuel Parra, wanted to make it more accessible to his colleagues teaching in Columbia where the case is set. So Juan provided us with the translation, which by the time you read this will be available through our distribution partners. We usually don't publish the Spanish version in the printed journal, but decided to this time in order to let our readers know that this is possible.

In talking about the unique portfolio of cases in this issue, we've highlighted three of the six cases. The other three cases are equally worthy of your consideration. So please look over the table of contents of this issue and consider using one or more of these cases in your courses, or perhaps even more significantly consider sharing the table of contents from this issue with your colleagues so they can see the interesting cases that will now be available for adoption through our numerous distribution partners, including Harvard, Ivey and The Case Centre.

We began this 'From the Editors' note by talking about the Editor transition that is in process. But there are other transitions happening as well. By the time that you read this, the *Case Research Journal* should be operating off of the ScholarOne platform. For a long time, the journal has operated on a custom system built and supported by Christian Ratterman. When Christian built the system, he was a student of then editor David Rosenthal in the early 2000s. The system and Christian have served us well for 15 years, but the time had come to migrate to the industry standard ScholarOne system with its 24/7 support system and state of the art security protocols. While there might be some short term inconvenience as we make this transition, there are real long term benefits of the move for NACRA and the CRJ. Thanks for your patience with the process. And by the time that you read this, NACRA and the CRJ will also likely have a new website, thanks to the leadership of NACRA co-presidents Kathy Savage and Jeff Shay. The new platform that we are building the website on is the same that we have been using for the annual meetings the last few years and should allow us to provide much more timely website updates. As with the move to ScholarOne, there will likely be a few issues that we will need to figure out in the coming months, but we hope that this move will allow us to maintain a more up to date and effective web presence.

Finally, we want to encourage all of you to submit your cases to the *Case Research Journal*. Publication in the CRJ provides you the broadest access to distribution and as such presents the greatest opportunity for your case to have real impact on the education of students around the globe. While our review process is quite rigorous, and we necessarily reject more cases than we can accept (our acceptance rate is about 20%), we work hard to turn around case reviews within about 60 days. That means within about 60 days of submission of your decision-focused case, you will have reviewer and editor feedback and a reasonable indication of the potential for your case to earn publication in the CRJ. We look forward to seeing your cases.

Sincerely

Gina Grandy, Editor
John Lawrence, Outgoing Editor
Case Research Journal

Contents

Entrepreneurship

- *Entrepreneurship*
- *Exit/Harvest*
- *New Ventures*
- *Online Retailing*

KickShot: Gooooooooooal!   1

Michael A. McCollough, University of Idaho [875 Perimeter Drive, MS 3161, Moscow, Idaho 83844-3161, mccollou@uidaho.edu]

Aziz Makhani, an entrepreneur who has developed and marketed the soccer board game KickShot, is evaluating two buyout offers against the option of continuing to market the game himself. The two offers mirror those common for many startups, a pure cash buyout versus an offer with a smaller amount up front but a royalty on future sales The case provides an opportunity to quantitatively and qualitatively evaluates the offers versus Aziz retaining ownership of the game and links the possible actions to Makhani's goals and objectives, including his personality. Within this context, the case highlights the need for an entrepreneur to have an exit, or harvest strategy from the very start.

Family Business Management

- *Family Business Management*
- *The Four Cs Model*
- *The Intention-based Model of Succession Planning*
- *Socioemotional Wealth in Family Firms*
- *Succession Financing*

Monmouth Rubber & Plastics   13

Stuart Rosenberg, Monmouth University [Leon Hess Business School, West Long Branch, NJ 07764-1898, srosenbe@monmouth.edu]

John Bonforte, the owner and president of Monmouth Rubber & Plastics, needed to decide whether to accept an offer from a potential buyer for the family business. Monmouth had been a successful company with a strong family culture since John founded it over forty years earlier. A number of risks had recently surfaced, however, that gave him reason for concern about the future of the business. His son, John Jr., had expressed an interest in taking over the business, but with a lucrative offer on the table, John needed to consider a variety of factors in order to make his decision.

Accounting

- *Accounting*
- *Internal control*
- *COSO Framework*
- *Fraud*
- *Management Compensation*

Houston We Have a Problem: They Paid Themselves Bonuses! 29

Pascale Lapointe-Antunes* and Deborah McPhee, Brock University [1812 Sir Isaac Brock Way, St. Catharines, Ontario, Canada, L2S 3A1, plapointe@brocku.ca]

Amanda Walsh's first year at Vanderville Plastics Company had been quite tumultuous. She had discovered that VPC's financial situation was precarious, and had witnessed a change in ownership, repeated requests for funding to the owners to help alleviate VPC's cash flow issues, and more recently, the sudden resignation of Peter Giroux, the company's CFO. Amanda had just realized to her great disbelief that the owners did not know about a recent payout of bonuses for the 2005 financial year. The case has students look at the events surrounding the payout as they unfold in the day-to-day life of Amanda to help them develop the professional judgment required to better interpret the oral assertions made by management, assess the risk of material misstatement due to fraud, and provide recommendations to improve a client organization's control environment and fraud risk management practices related to incentive compensation and management override of controls.

- *Accounting*
- *Short-Term Decision Making*
- *Marginal Revenue/Cost*
- *Agricultural Production*
- *Relevancy of Information*

Arkansas Egg Company: Cracks in the Specialty Egg Market 45

David G. Hyatt, University of Arkansas [354 Business Building, 1 University of Arkansas, Fayetteville, AR 72701, dhyatt@uark.edu]

Michael Cox, CEO of the Arkansas Egg Company (AEC), must decide what to do about 130,000 hens producing organic cage-free eggs (specialty eggs) on company farms near the small town of Summers, Arkansas. His margins for these eggs had been protected under a contract, but on October 1, 2016 that contract would expire in highly unfavorable market conditions. Late summer 2016 market conditions were rough because the overall supply of conventional white eggs was high relative to demand, depressing prices and negatively affecting consumer demand for specialty eggs. The contract expiration meant AEC would compete in an open market where specialty eggs were selling below his variable production cost. Cox must decide whether to minimize his losses by euthanizing the hens or to try to hang on a while longer hoping for a market rebound in the fourth quarter. Student's complete a marginal cost / marginal revenue analysis and consider non-financial factors to make a recommendation.

Finance

- *Finance*
- *Capital Budgeting*
- *Project Evaluation*
- *Retailing*
- *Financial Analysis*

Murphy Stores: Capital Projects   **53**

John S. Strong, College of William and Mary [Raymond A. Mason School of Business, 101 Ukrop Way, Williamsburg, Virginia 23187-8795, john.strong@mason.wm.edu]

The Head of Capital Planning at Murphy Stores, a large multibrand retailer, is facing limited remaining funds in the company's capital budget, and is trying to choose between two projects. The first project involves adoption of RFID technology in the company's department and/or hardware stores to help reduce merchandise theft. The second project is to install more energy-efficient lighting in stores. The two projects have very different characteristics in terms of their metrics, their risks, and the variability in their potential outcomes. The Capital Planning team is required to undertake full project evaluations, including cost of capital, net present value and internal rate of return, as well as extensive sensitivity and scenario analysis. The evaluation will serve as the basis for a recommendation to the company's senior executives serving on the Capital Committee.

Ethics & Corporate Social Responsibility

- *Corporate Social Responsibility*
- *Socially Responsible Marketing*
- *Business Ethics*
- *Public-Private partnerships*
- *Branding*
- *Cause Marketing*

La Campaña de Marketing de Oilcorp: **61**
Reacciones Mixtas a una Iniciativa de Responsabilidad Social

Juan M. Parra, Inalde Business School [Campus U. Sabana, Autopista Norte, Km. 7, Costado Occ, Chía, Colombia, juanm.parra@inalde.edu.co]

The Colombian Red Cross approached Oilcorp, owner of the largest regional chain of service stations in the country, requesting its participation in its 100th anniversary celebration with a brand awareness campaign for its social programs. Given that the annual budget had already been approved without this campaign in mind, Oilcorp's CEO assigned the task of raising money to the Marketing Department. They opted for a small donation per gallon sold during the month of May and asking customers to provide personal information to be added to Oilcorp's database, making it clear that Oilcorp, in exchange, would contribute more money to the Colombian Red Cross. Nevertheless, the campaign backfired. For many, it seemed that the company was taking advantage of a social cause for marketing purposes. Consequently, the marketing team needed to decide what actions to take, given that the campaign was not on track to meet stakeholder's expectations. [Note: This case is the Spanish-language version of the case 'Oilcorp's Marketing Campaign: Mixed Reactions to a CSR Initiative' that appeared in the *Case Research Journal*, Volume 37 Issue 4.]

KickShot: GOOOOOOOOOAL!

Michael A. McCollough, University of Idaho

Aziz Makhani leaned back in his office chair and checked the online sales of his soccer board game KickShot! on Amazon.com. As of May 31, 2016, his year-to-date selling was 1,928 units. At this pace, he should easily exceed his 2015 sales of 4,000 units. Further, he was on track to record his highest earnings since he started KickShot in 2013.

The question was simple: what to do next? Before him were buyout offers from two of the top board game companies in the world. TKG offered him a flat $250,000 for the rights to KickShot. HB[1] offered him $75,000 up front with a royalty of 6% of sales for the subsequent five years, up to a maximum of 500,000 units with a minimum of 2,000 total units guaranteed. Both companies wanted an answer by September 30, 2016. If he did not accept either offer, he could continue to market the game himself, building on what should be his best year ever.

"What should I do?" he wondered. From the start, Makhani's goal was to sell or license the game for "six figures." Contemplating the offers he wondered which he should accept. But in the back of his mind he wondered if he might be selling out too early and just how far he could take KickShot on his own? How, in the words of sportscaster Andrés Cantor, was the best way to score the game winning Goooooooooooooooal! with KickShot?

AZIZ MAKHANI AND KICKSHOT

As a boy growing up in Myanmar (formerly Burma), Makhani was obsessed with football, what most in the United States called soccer. He learned the sport playing with his friends in the streets of his hometown of Mandalay, Burma's second largest city. Makhani emigrated to the U.S. in 1971 to attend college, earning a Bachelor of Science in Electrical Engineering from the University of Texas. Following this, Makhani worked as a Quality Engineer. While still working full time he earned his Master's in Electrical Engineering from the University of Southern California followed by a Masters of Business Administration (MBA) from Long Beach State University. After earning his MBA, Makhani worked in a variety of technology companies, gradually gravitating toward startups where he assumed more managerial than engineering duties. Settling down in a small college town in the Pacific Northwest, Makhani became a U.S. citizen, had a family, and worked at a number of area technology companies.

While life had taken Makhani to the other side of the world from his birthplace, he never lost his passion for soccer. Makhani served as a volunteer youth soccer referee, progressing to club and high school matches, and ultimately achieved his certified soccer referee status. The kids he watched lived up to the cliché of U.S. soccer players. As Makhani put it, "They work hard and are physically adept, but they simply do not understand the game – not just the rules and the hand signals of the referee, but the strategy and tactics of the game." Makhani wondered if a kid's game might not be the way to teach them a greater understanding of soccer. One night Makhani awoke with a vision for a soccer game that would be no more difficult than Uno[2]. Almost simultaneously in 2012, the local tech startup where he had served as the director of marketing closed its doors. Makhani felt, at age 59, that the time was right to launch his own venture, one that combined his love of board games with his love of soccer.

KickShot was targeted at very young players (ages 5-12). Makhani hired an artist to illustrate the game with colorful cartoon animal characters (see Figure 1, next page) which focus groups results showed to be very popular with young people. The characters in the cards were illustrations of endangered species as players and referees (allowing a twofold education mission – soccer and endangered animals from around the world). Each player had a name and biography. The intent of the game was to be engaging, entertaining, and educational.

For a time, KickShot was Makhani's full time job. However, in March 2015 he accepted a position as the Business Development Advisor at a state Small Business Development Center (SBDC). Makhani enjoyed working with other entrepreneurs, but his new career opportunity was demanding and kept him very busy. As Makhani told a friend when discussing the offers, "I am passionate about helping entrepreneurs, sharing my experience in the local community; the job is a perfect fit. If these buyout offers had not come along, things might be different, but early exit allows me to focus on helping local entrepreneurs and teach classes. It's not always about the money."

Soccer in the U.S.

According to the U.S. Youth Soccer organization, there were only 103,432 registered youth soccer players in 1974. In the mid 1990's, the number of players increased significantly, and by 2014 the number was 3,055,148, with an almost even split between boys and girls[3]. Federation Internationale de Football Association (FIFA), the governing body of the sport, reported that soccer was the most popular sport in the world with 265 million players. The U.S. trailed only China with 24,473,000 players registered with the U.S. Soccer Federation.[4]

Viewership of soccer in the U.S. had also increased. In 2006, the FIFA World Cup attracted an estimated 17 million total viewers, higher than the 15.8 million estimated to have viewed the 2006 World Series.[5] In 2010, World Cup viewership increased 22% over 2006, while in 2014, the USA-Portugal match attracted 18.2 million viewers.[6]

Figure 1: KickShot and Aziz Makhani

Source. Makhani, A. (2016).

THE BOARD GAME INDUSTRY

Perhaps somewhat paradoxically in an era of electronic gaming, the board game industry experienced excellent growth. From 2010 to 2014, annual board game purchases increased between 25% and 40% each year.[7] This success was driven by independent game designers and publishers who were producing games that millennial consumers found fun to play. Examples of fun and innovative board games launched by independent entrepreneurs included Ugg-Tect (gamers build 3D structures while communicating only in grunts and hitting opponents with inflatable clubs), Pandemic (in which players try to rid the planet of deadly infectious diseases), Dead of Winter (players attempt to avoid being eaten by Zombies), and Freedom – The Underground Railroad (players sheltered runaway slaves in pre-Civil War America.). Hasbro was the largest seller of board games with such well-known brands as Monopoly, Scrabble, and Clue, yet it only held a 20% market share. Therefore, the industry was not highly concentrated and smaller and independent board game developers drove sales.[8] In 2013, board game developers raised $52.1 million via Kickstarter while video game developers raised $45.3 million during the same period.[9] Significantly, many of these board game developers choose to remain independent, rejecting lucrative buyout offers while growing their business in terms of sales and profitability. As Peter Blenkharn, cofounder of Inside the Box Games (maker of independent/indie games Statecraft, Sub Terra, and Molecular) stated, "Publishing your own games is definitely profitable, the profit margins are enormous on medium runs and there's a huge amount of room for more indie publishers." [10]

Internet and smartphone gaming stimulated sales of board games, as consumers downloaded cheap or free versions of games to try out before they bought the more expensive board games. Compared to PC, Xbox, and PlayStation games, board games were generally seen as less expensive and more fun for the entire family than video games. Online retailers aggregated and provided a large number of board games with customer reviews, reviving a category largely ignored or downplayed by large "big-box" retailers. Even as the mobile gaming industry struggled to come up with the next Candy Crush, Farmville, or Angry Birds, sales of board games on Amazon increased by double digits from 2012 to 2013 and sales at U.S. game and hobby stores increased 15% to 20% per year from 2011 - 2013[11]. Even the summer of 2016 hit, augmented reality game Pokémon, could be traced to a simple collectable card game.

DEVELOPING AND LAUNCHING KICKSHOT

After his 2012 epiphany, Makhani performed a preliminary assessment that focused on the current competition in the marketplace, discovering that while there were soccer board games and electronic soccer games, none were targeted at young players. He gave his KickShot prototype to gamers, watched them play, and solicited feedback. Over several iterations, the game evolved from a simple card game to a board game with multiple levels allowing KickShot to appeal to very young players as well as the entire family.

Makhani developed a business plan that outlined how he would market the game, his estimated required resources, how long it would take to reach the market, and his exit strategy of selling or licensing the game. He also established a network of advisors, friends, and potential investors who were excited about KickShot and highly engaged, which he could turn to, not just for financial help if needed, but advice and guidance. Makhani avoided angel investors, venture capitalists, crowdfunding, and any individuals he did not know personally. This was primarily because he did not want to lose control of his venture but also because he realized that raising funds from those he did not know personally would be time-consuming. Indeed, Makhani feared he would end up spending all his time raising money and not developing and marketing the game. He shared with a colleague, "Based on my prior experience working for start-ups, I realized that once I had outside investors I would be spending a significant amount of time simply interacting with these individuals, providing financial, marketing, and other updates."

Makhani also felt it was important to develop his credibility and demonstrate demand via sales, before seeking out investments from others. As KickShot progressed, he could go back to his network of advisors, show that he was making headway, and seek financial support if needed. In 2013, one of his advisors offered Makhani a $50,000, 3% interest loan. While Makhani did not need the funds at that time, the offer was still on the table if needed. Makhani sought and received in-kind investments. Others offered furniture, services, and advice.

Makhani was unable to find a domestic producer of the game that would provide timely and affordable quotes for his low initial production runs. Therefore he manufactured the game in Taiwan. His neighbor who had offered the $50,000 loan was a successful entrepreneur and offered to warehouse product and volunteered his company's expertise in shipping and importing, cutting 2/3 of the cost of shipping KickShot from Taiwan where it was produced.

EXTENDED PRODUCT MIX

Simultaneous with the 2013 launch of the KickShot board game Makhani also released a line of accessories, including washable placemats (set of four for $12.00), inspirational/motivational posters ($5.00 each), and water bottles ($1.50) that featured the colorful cartoon characters. While accessories had very high margins, they accounted for only about 5% of sales in 2016.

Makhani's mobile strategy involved sponsoring students at a local university to develop the initial app as their senior class project. Version 1 was a free app, which allowed users to roll virtual dice and was launched in May of 2014 as a free download on Android platforms. Through September 2014, the game was downloaded 1,300 times with feedback suggesting changes to make the game better. Version 1 was, as Makhani put it "Not a very good game." Version 2, which was still in development as of May 2016 would employ virtual cards, some AI (artificial intelligence), and would remain a free download. Version 3, which was not yet in development was envisioned to have significant AI and was planned to retail at 99 cents. All of the apps were/would be in java script and operating system independent so they could be "ported" to Apple products. Using senior class projects kept his costs low, but the speed to market was poor. Having version 3 professionally developed would likely cost approximately $5,000.

KickShot had full copyright and trademark protection which covered the game rules and cartoon characters. While Makhani worried that someone might "knock off his game" requiring costly litigation, his primary concern was that someone might introduce a soccer game that while similar was distinct enough that it would not infringe on his intellectual property (IP). Makhani felt that he had a ten years remaining of strong IP protection.

PRICE

KickShot was initially priced to retail at $24.95. The manufacturing cost of the game was $9.50 with shipping bringing the final cost to $13.00. The more games Makhani ordered at a time, the better the cost. At the $9.50 cost, Makhani had to purchase in lots of 1,000 to 5,000. However, if he ordered 5,000 units or more, his costs would drop by 24%.

RETAILING KICKSHOT

KickShot was sold in 32 physical "brick and mortar" stores at the close of 2014, his second year in business. Makhani approached Costco in 2014 and was told that "board games don't sell." He had not met with Wal-Mart or Toys R Us. Simply attending a trade show where he might catch the attention of one of these chains would cost $5,000. Makhani knew that only about 2% of new suppliers that applied to Wal-Mart were accepted and of that number very few were successful enough to remain on the shelves over the long run. Against his low probability of success were the significant demands involving cost, packaging, shipping, and inventory management that a large chain would demand.

Makhani realized early the potential of the Internet to achieve national distribution without the challenges of establishing a brick and mortar presence through small independents or large chains. For online sales, he initially focused on offering the game via his own website, kickshot.org. He also offered the game on eBay which yielded no sales. Amazon accounted for the majority of his sales. KickShot started selling on Amazon in the fall of 2013 at a retail price of $24.95. For every sale, Amazon took a cut of $9.35, leaving a net gross margin of $2.60 after his cost for the game of $13.00. Further, in order to gain exposure, Makhani began to sell via an Amazon agent, The Escape Place, in early 2014. Agents enhanced search results given their power rating and because they sold a large line up of products. In addition, the agent helped Makhani learn how to maximize sales on Amazon. Since using the agent, sales of KickShot on Amazon increased significantly. However, this agent also took a commission. As a result, Makhani increased the retail price of KickShot to $28.95. He found that unit sales seemed unaffected by the price increase, leading him to believe that his target was relatively price insensitive. With this new retail of $28.95, and after deducting the cost of manufacturing and shipping KickShot, paying Amazon fees, and his agent fees Makhani realized a net gross margin of $1.95 per game.

Makhani was required to keep a stock of games in the Amazon warehouse which was used to fulfill games sold under his own storefront (Sports Cards and Games). Makhani shipped games to his agent (adding an additional shipping cost), who was also required to keep an inventory at Amazon. Makhani was charged by Amazon a nominal inventory/storage fee for this required service which totaled less than $50 since 2013. Further, Amazon charged their total fee in part based on the weight ($1.59 for the first two pounds plus 39 cents a pound for each additional pound) and the physical size of the game. For instance, KickShot weighed 2.3 lbs. Amazon charged him for 3 lbs. This shipping charge was included in the total of $9.35 that Amazon charged per unit sale. (See Table 1 for a full detail of Amazon per unit fees.) On Amazon, sales were about 35% from Makhani and 65% via The Escape Place. However, all the games sold through Amazon, whether via Makhani or his agent, were warehoused and *Fulfilled by Amazon.com* (FBA) with free two-day prime shipping.

Table 1 – Amazon.com Fees $28.95 Retail Price

Fee Type	Amount
Amazon referral fee	$4.34/15% retail selling price
Per Item Listing fee	$.99
FBA (Fulfilled by Amazon) Fees	
Order Handling	$1.00
Pick and Pack	$1.04
Weight Handling	$1.98
FBA Total Fee	$4.02
Total Amazon Fees	$9.35

Source. Company documents (2015).

Purchases via KickShot.org were more profitable, yielding the best margin. The retail price on KickShot.org was $24.95 bringing the total price to the consumer with shipping in-line with Amazon. His website received good traffic, with 5,000 unique visitors a month with 60% visiting multiple pages. However, sales via KickShot.org had become negligible since he listed on Amazon.com, averaging only one or two games a quarter. Indeed, the conversion rate of visitors visiting his website that actually purchased the game via KickShot.org was below 1%.

At the start of 2016 he decided to eliminate all brick and mortar sales and focus exclusively on online sales. At the same time, feeling he had learned enough, Makhani ended his relationship with The Escape Place and began selling exclusively through his Amazon store front.

PROMOTION

With a limited amount of funds available, Makhani focused on inexpensive, cost effective promotional efforts. Starting in May of 2013 he visited gaming tournaments to promote his game and generate word-of-mouth. He also visited many physical retail outlets to gain shelf space and often visited stores to sell the game personally. Makhani believed his single most effective promotional tool was the Internet. If a consumer Googled soccer board games, KickShot was one of the top results. Further, his placement on Amazon helped drive consumers to his game. In addition to his webpage, Kickshot.org, Makhani also had a youtube.com channel with 122 videos, as well as a Facebook, Pinterest, and Twitter page. Makhani said, "I really used reviews, and I created videos that were fun to watch. I engaged with a World Cup coach and referee who also became my mentor. This individual wrote a widely followed blog; he posted about KickShot, and I reposted those blog comments to my own various social media platforms."

THE CUSTOMER

Sales on Amazon yielded interesting information about the customer and consumer. Games bought as gifts would often include a short message. From this, and by looking to see if the ship to address differed from the billing address, Makhani estimated that 60% of his sales were gifts, most from grandparents (the customer) to their grandkids (the consumer). In reflecting on the other 40% of his game sales, Makhani believed it was driven by millennials. These consumers were not just driving the resurgence of indie board games, but they turned to KickShot to enhance their kid's soccer skills.

INTERNATIONAL

Board gaming enjoyed an international audience. The Settlers of Catan, a game designed by a German dental technician sold 18 million copies since its release in 1995.[12] Soccer, as the world's most popular game, provided an opportunity for KickShot to expand internationally. A handful of customers in international markets sought out the game on Amazon and purchased it. However, there were specifically targeted online stores for international markets, including Amazon's international division. While Amazon had ten international marketplaces including China, Makhani felt that it would make the most sense to move into Europe first. There were some costs associated with going into Europe via Amazon. Some modification of the game (translated instructions) would be necessary, but Makhani lived in a community with two large universities with many foreign language instructors and international students. Therefore, obtaining translation services would be straightforward and relatively inexpensive. Makhani estimated these costs as approximately $6,000. Europe had a Value Added Tax (VAT) which was about 20% and would be added to the retail price. On the whole, Amazon fees for selling in Europe would be similar to those he already incurred in the U.S. Given how popular soccer was in Europe, Makhani believe that he should be able to at least double his total sales every year from 2017 to 2020, with European sales equaling U.S. sales by 2020.

PROFITABILITY AND FINANCIAL CONDITION

The Balance Sheet and Income Statement for Sports Cards and Games are provided in Tables 2 and 3 on the following page. For fiscal year ended 2013, 2014, and 2015, revenues were $8,775, $23,956, and $23,696 respectively. For fiscal year 2016, estimated sales through June 30 were approximately $46,304 (Table 3). Sales were seasonal for KickShot, with approximately 40% of all revenue in the fourth quarter and the remaining sales generally spread more or less equally over the other three quarters. Domestic shipping costs covered the shipping from the port to Makhani and from Makhani to Amazon, and he expected it to continue to average around 4% of sales (international shipping costs of $3.50 were included in cost of goods sold and Amazon fees included their shipping costs.) Web hosting and marketing, office supplies/help, and travel were about 0.1% of sales, but it was anticipated that these costs would rise to around 1% per category going forward. Current inventory was $2,200. KickShot had total cash on hand of $6,450 with liabilities of $2,200. Makhani retained 100 percent of the equity of the company. As Makhani contemplated his future in mid-2016, he felt confident that if he needed additional financial backing, it could be obtained. Further, KickShot was itself generating significant positive cash flow.

Table 2: Sports Cards and Games Balance Sheet as of July 31, 2016

Assets			Liabilities and Owner's Equity		
Current Assets			Current Liabilities		
Cash	$6,450		Income taxes payable	$2,200	
Inventory	2,200		Total Current Liabilities		$2,200
Total Current Assets		$8,650			
			Long-Term Liabilities		
Fixed Long-Term Assets			Long-Term debt	0	
Intangible Assets	0		Total Long Term Liabilities		0
Total Fixed Assets		0			
			Owner's Equity: Retained Earnings		$6,450
Total Assets		**$8,650**			
			Total Liabilities & Owner's Equity		**$8,650**

Source: Company documents (2016).

Table 3: Sports Cards and Games Income Statement
For the Years Ending December 31, 2013, 2014, 2015 and partial year 2016 and estimated half-year (June 30) 2016

Revenue	2013	2014	2015	2016
Revenues from Brick & Mortar	1,316	1,450	0	0
Revenues from Amazon	7,459	9,275	11,138	46,304
Revenues from The Escape Place	0	13,231	12,558	0
Total Revenues	8,775	23,956	23,696	46,304
Expenses				
Cost of Goods Sold	5,175	17,653	17,423	30,173
Domestic Shipping	675	2,302	2,272	1,870
Web hosting and Marketing	52	78	78	40
Office Supplies/Help	48	65	54	40
Travel	64	88	76	50
Total Expenses	6,014	20,186	19,903	32,173
Net Income Before Taxes	2,761	3,770	3,793	14,131
Income Tax Expense	828	1,131	1,138	2,107
Net Income	1,933	2,639	2,655	12,024

Note: All fees associated with selling on Amazon and The Escape Place is reflected in lower revenues.

Source. Company documents (2016)

Makhani's exit strategy from the very start was to sell or license KickShot to a partner that would be able to move much more aggressively than Makhani, landing shelf space at large chain stores. Further, the buyer could use its significant size to gain economies of scale in production to bring down production costs and the retail price. There was ample evidence of board games being developed by inventors which were subsequently bought by large companies and Makhani always hoped to get enough sales to demonstrate KickShot's viability to a large company and justify a "six-figure deal." While Makhani developed KickShot to educate young people about soccer (and endangered animals), he did not feel that "selling out" would negate this goal. To the contrary, a large game company could leverage its resources to put the game into the hands of more players than he ever could. Therefore, licensing was a win-win in his eyes. Now, with the two offers before him, he found that his initial exit strategy could be realized. But he wondered if he was being hasty, if he could do better on his own, or if he worked to improve sales and profitability he might be able to get a better offer in a couple of years.

The offers came shortly after Makhani had attended a gaming show in Seattle, Washington in early 2016. Makhani was visited by representatives of TKG and HB. After some back and forth, Makhani was able to significantly increase the proposals to the point that he felt he had the best offers he was going to receive. But were the offers strong enough or should he continue to market the game on his own? He took out a pad of paper and began to organize his thoughts.

The first offer from TKG for $250,000 ($150,000 in year one, and $100,000 in year two) was the most straightforward. The offer would allow him to turn a nice profit on the game. Makhani, in discussing the offers with a friend, said "It would allow me to clear a bit over my investment, if you add up all the costs, manufacturing tooling, my time and effort; I should clear $70,000, maybe a bit more." KickShot, after consuming five years of his life, would simply no longer be his concern. Further, Makhani like most entrepreneurs already had several new ventures that he was mulling over. He felt he could turn his experience gained from KickShot to develop new board games. TKG (or HB) might buy the rights to any new game(s). Alternatively, he was considering a smartphone app that would allow anyone to find a bathroom anyplace. Other ideas included an app to help customers find their seats in arenas, and a navigator to help college students find their classrooms on large campuses. The $250,000 would provide the capital to pursue these or other new venture he could dream up.

The second offer from HB called for an upfront payment of $75,000 with a royalty of 6% on unit sales of up to 500,000 (within five years) with 2,000 units guaranteed. At current retail, it would take board game sales of just over 100,000 or 20,000 a year over the five years to equal the TKG offer. While well above his current annual sales, Makhani felt the number was clearly realistic given HB's marketing power. They could achieve placement of the game in large chain retailers' brick and mortar stores and on their online marketplaces and they could move into multiple international marketplaces. Wal-Mart alone had 3,946 Supercenters and discount stores in the U.S., with a total of 6,369 international stores.[13] Target and Toys R Us would add thousands more potential retail outlets. Therefore, if HB marketed the game, the 500,000 unit sales over five years was realistic. With volume production, HB might lower the game production cost and the unit retail, probably to $19.99, further increasing the likely unit sales but reducing his overall dollar royalty per game. Further, there was a clause in the contract that said all derivative products developed by HB would not be covered under the royalty agreement. Most obviously, this meant any future apps or online games. But what if HB significantly modified the game, perhaps changing the rules or the characters and then argued that this was a new and different game? While Makhani did not think this would happen, he could not rule it out. Of greater concern was that they might just "shelve" the game and not actively pursue commercialization. Makhani had seen this happen before, where an inventor licensed a product and ultimately received little to no royalty revenue from sales. The reasons why this happened were varied. Sometimes, the company had a competing product in the works and wanted to clear the way by eliminating competition with a buyout offer. Sometimes, it proved more difficult to commercialize the opportunity than envisioned. Or it could simply turn out that other new products in HB's pipeline would turn out to be more promising. Makhani would have little leverage to see that the game was actively marketed. Still, what if HB really did ramp up selling and ran with the game? When his friend asked him over coffee what he thought the likelihood of HB aggressively marketing the game and not just sitting on it was he replied "50/50, I think."

Makhani could also turn down both offers and keep marketing the game himself. His friend and neighbor still had the $50,000 loan offer on the table. This would provide the resources for Makhani to take KickShot to the next level. He could order in larger volume to get a lower unit price. With a lower price and more margin per unit, he could aggressively pursue online international sales. Having eliminated the agent, Makhani was now earning more per game, and he was not seeing a reduction in sales. The most straightforward way to evaluate going it alone would be to assume lower costs by buying in bulk, not using an agent, and opening a European Amazon storefront. How many unit sales would he need to turn down the TKG and HB offers, and was that level of sales realistic he wondered? However, if he did decide to stay the course and turn down the offers, what would TKG and HB do then? They clearly saw the opportunity of a soccer board game. It seemed unlikely that they would abandon the field, or rather in this case, the pitch, if Makhani did not sell.

He wondered "what should I do?" What was the best way to score the decisive GOOOOOOOOOOOOOOOOOOOAL!!!!!!!!!!!!!!!!!!!!!

NOTES

[1] Due to confidentiality concerns, TKG and HB are pseudonyms to disguise the names of the real companies.

[2] Uno is a best-selling Mattel card game for ages seven and up.

[3] Key Statistics/Membership Statistics. Retrieved December 11, 2017 from http://www.usyouthsoccer.org/media_kit/keystatistics/

[4] Kunz, M. (2007, July). 265 million playing football. Retrieved December 11, 2017, from http://www.fifa.com/mm/document/fifafacts/bcoffsurv/emaga_9384_10704.pdf

[5] Sandomir, R. (2006, July 11). Cup ratings are up, but fans deserve better. Retrieved December 11, 2017 from http://www.nytimes.com/2006/07/11/sports/soccer/11sandomir.html?_r=0In 2010 112

[6] Murray, C. (2014, July 2). U.S. Soccer world cup viewing party – USMNT vs Belgium. Retrieved December 11, 2017 from http://www.sbisoccer.com/2014/07/americans-digital-experience.html

[7] Owen D. (2014, November 25). Board games' golden age: sociable, brilliant and driven by the internet. Retrieved December 11, 2017 from http://www.theguardian.com/technology/2014/nov/25/board-games-internet-playstation-xbox

[8] Hudak, M. (2016, March 31). Board games are gaining momentum in 2016. Retrieved December 11, 2017 from http://www.globaltoynews.com/2016/03/board-games-are-gaining-momentum-in-2016.html

[9] Wingfield, N. (2014, May 5). High-tech push has board games rolling again. Retrieved December 11, 2017 from https://www.nytimes.com/2014/05/06/technology/high-tech-push-has-board-games-rolling-again.html

[10] Martin, T. (2017, January 23). How board games became a billion-dollar business. Retrieved December 11, 2017 from http://www.newstatesman.com/culture/games/2017/01/how-board-games-became-billion-dollar-business

[11] Board game statistics. Retrieved December 11, 2017 from https://infogram.com/board_game_statistics

[12] Teuber, K. Information about Klaus Teuber. Retrieved Decebmer 11, 2017 from http://www.catan.com/about-us/klaus-teuber

[13] Our locations. Retrieved December 11, 2017 from http://corporate.walmart.com/our-story/locations/united-states#/

Monmouth Rubber & Plastics

NACRA
NORTH AMERICAN CASE
RESEARCH ASSOCIATION

Stuart Rosenberg, Monmouth University

It was an overcast morning in late September 2008, and John Bonforte was having lunch with his son, John Jr., at the Turning Point, a popular restaurant in the Pier Village community of Long Branch, New Jersey. John, 67, was the owner and president of Monmouth Rubber & Plastics Corporation, a Long Branch manufacturing company that he had founded forty four years earlier. He was unusually quiet, staring out the window at the crashing waves of the Atlantic Ocean across the boardwalk from the restaurant.

"Dad," John Jr. said, "what do you think about the offer that came in yesterday for the business?"

John looked his son directly in the eyes. "It's a very good offer – $5.5 million."

John Jr., who was 36, stroked his beard anxiously. "Maybe we should hold off."

"Our sales have slowed down, son. The economy probably isn't going to turn around for a long time."

"I realize that", John Jr. said.

John smiled. "This might be the right time to cash out and sell the business. You know that a lot of companies are taking their business overseas." He paused for a moment, and then continued. "What worries me more, I think, is the city's redevelopment zone. I don't know how the courts are going to rule on the challenge to eminent domain."

"Well, if the developers force us out, we do have the Riverside building as a fallback," John Jr. said, lifting his cup for a sip of his coffee. "That would help to take care of our staff. After all, they're family to us."

ALL IN THE FAMILY

John Bonforte was raised in Long Branch. He started in the rubber industry in 1961 when he took a job at the New York City sales office of Rubatex Corporation, one of the largest rubber manufacturers in the world. While at Rubatex, he learned the business, holding various positions in sales, marketing, and product development.

After he helped develop a new product for the company, he convinced his manager in 1964 to allow him to service small customers as a side job. He would purchase rubber from Rubatex and take it to his uncle's cellar in Long Branch, where he cut the rubber and sold it to the small customers that the firm could not service from their large factory. Soon the side job became such a success that John decided to keep the business, which he named Monmouth Rubber & Plastics, as a full time venture. At first the company started out as a fabricator, slicing rubber into shapes and selling it to other businesses, but in 1971 John decided to begin manufacturing his own rubber. He moved the factory to a couple of different locations before settling on its current site in Long Branch, two blocks from the ocean.

The city of Long Branch was very supportive of John's company. "Long Branch has been a big help in encouraging us to be here and stay here and grow here," he always said.

After being married briefly to his first wife, John met his second wife, Barbara, and together they raised a blended family. Between them, they had four children – Kelly, Scott, John Jr., and Kristin – each of whom was adopted. All four children were born between 1969 and 1973, and they all worked in the business from an early age.

Eventually, three of the four children moved on to other careers. Kelly became a fourth grade teacher in nearby Rumson, while Scott and Kristin became co-owners of the popular Long Branch eatery, Fa Nagle the Bagel. Only John Jr. remained with the company. After graduating from the University of Rhode Island, John Jr. worked at a couple of other firms for a few years before returning to work at Monmouth full time. His father took him under his wing, and John Jr. soon became the company's sales manager.

The grandchildren would also begin to work in the business, gaining valuable life experience along the way. John treated them in the workplace using the same "firm but fair" approach that he had used for their parents. One example of this approach was when he reprimanded his grandson, Max, who had begun to come to the factory after school. In the beginning, Max didn't appear to be cooperative to some of the employees. John sat Max down and explained to him that even though he was only fourteen, what he did at the factory mattered. Another example of this approach was how John handled his sixteen year old granddaughter, Missy, after she didn't come in to help out in the office as she had promised. He firmly explained to her the consequence of her not showing up without notice, and then he told her he loved her. By consistently instilling the value of a strong work ethic in his family, he was able to secure their unshakable respect.[1]

Early on, John ensured that the cornerstone of his business would be based on family values. The company employed over forty people. Each employee was considered to be part of the Bonfortes' extended family. "Our people are the engine that gives life to our company," John would say with pride. (See Exhibit 1 for a group photo of Monmouth's employees.)

Bernard, a machine operator, and Carlos, a quality control manager, represent two examples of how much Monmouth cared about people.

One night in 1975, Bernard walked up to John on the street and said he was in desperate need of a job to support his young family. John said that he could come to the factory the next day, but only if he was serious about working. Thirty-three years later, Bernard was still working for Monmouth.

The second example took place about thirty years later. Carlos was employed by Monmouth when he was asked to return home to his native Bolivia to take care of serious family issues. He was not able to return to the United States until two years later. During that time, the company continued to give him contracted work and kept the door open for him until he came back.

Exhibit 1. Monmouth Rubber & Plastics

Source: Monmouth Rubber & Plastics

Approximately 70 percent of the employees had been with the company for over ten years. Monmouth had no union. The factory ran 24 hours a day with two shifts: 7 a.m. to 7 p.m., and 7 p.m. to 7 a.m. With a smaller, less experienced staff working nights, Monmouth was careful what jobs they ran on the second shift.

The organization structure was relatively flat, which helped foster a family environment. Reporting directly to John were the operations manager, sales manager, and office manager. Production was supervised by a quality manager, a product manager, and a value added manager[2], each of whom reported directly to the operations manager; because the organization was small enough, however, production staff were encouraged to come to either John or John Jr. at any time. (See Exhibit 2 on the next page for Monmouth's organizational chart.)

Although John Jr. was one of the three direct reports to John, Monmouth's staff and its customers recognized that he was the number two person in the company. John Jr. had come to have as much of an affinity for the business as his dad, and father and son were very close. Increasingly, John Jr. had recommended to his father strategic positions with regard to the direction that Monmouth should take. John Jr. had begun to express to John that he would be interested in taking over the family business at some point in the future. With John showing no signs of slowing down, the notion of a formal transfer of ownership was never articulated to employees or customers. John Jr. was unfailingly deferential to his father and he refrained from discussing the topic of family succession with anyone else.

Exhibit 2. Monmouth Rubber & Plastics Organization Chart

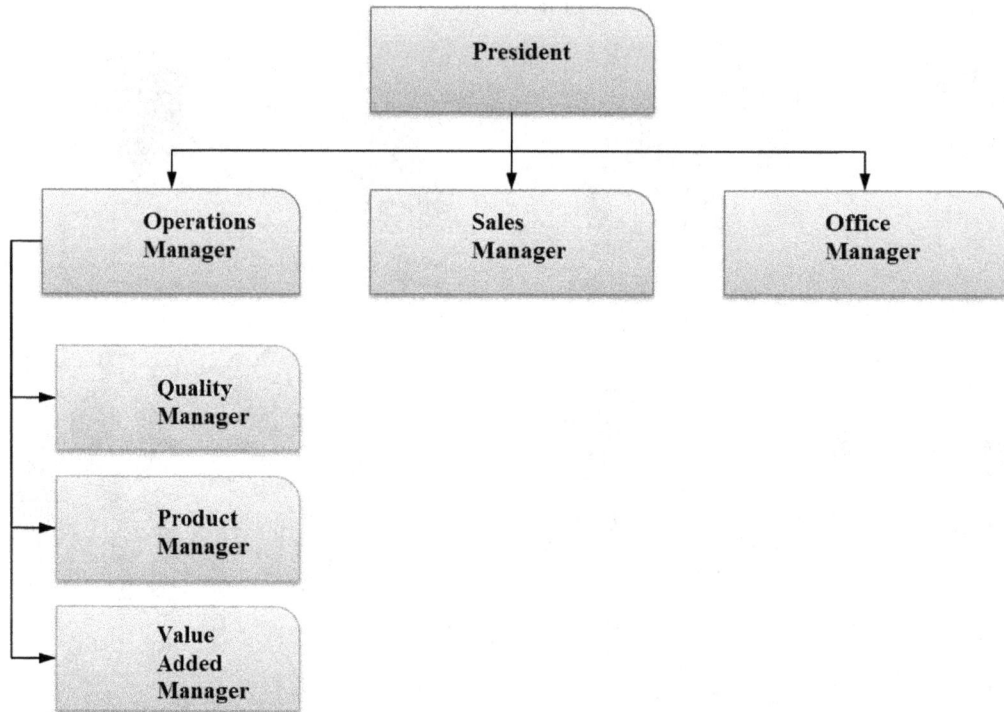

Source: Monmouth Rubber & Plastics

The family culture of the business was exemplified by its weekly meeting of the president and each of Monmouth's six managers. John was very amiable, and the firm's managers also characterized John Jr. this way. John made sure that the meeting was always run informally, combining time dedicated to the needs of the business along with time dedicated to catching up with each of the managers on their lives outside the business.

Each of the managers was trained in customer-oriented and market-driven principles. Monmouth's willingness to develop new products helped to keep the company relevant and not just a commodity supplier. John believed that the family relationship that he was able to nurture with his customers was something that a larger business might not be able to cultivate.

An example of Monmouth's relationship with its customers was provided in the following testimonial by Ron Rudolph, the owner of a St. Louis fabricating company:

> We convert about 4,000 different raw materials from various manufacturers to make parts such as gaskets for our customers, such as GE and Whirlpool that make products like refrigerators, washing machines, and vacuum cleaners. We don't make exclusive deals with our suppliers. We do business with the suppliers that give us the best service. Monmouth supplies us with sponge rubber, which is 20 to 25 percent of our business. Monmouth makes life easy for me. There are never any delivery problems, there are never any quality issues, and there aren't any price fluctuations. There is no haggling; we do it all on a handshake. John has also been a huge help with technical support. He

helps me a lot with questions that my customers have for their product needs – even if it's not related to something that Monmouth makes.

John understood how important it was to build a strong bond with his customers. "The one thing that drives this business most," he would say, "is the family culture at its core." With its mission to emphasize the importance of family over the bottom line, John was confident that the firm's broader measures of success would also lead to bottom line success.

John had started his business as a labor of love, but it would become a model for other fledgling private businesses in the Long Branch area. In building strong relationships with its employees as well as its customers, Monmouth clearly kept it all in the family.

THE MANUFACTURING OF RUBBER

Rubber is an elastic material obtained from latex, which is the milky sap of the rubber tree. Although its exact origin is unknown, the indigenous people of the Americas had known and used latex long before the arrival of European explorers. Christopher Columbus observed the Mayan people use the substance to roll into balls for their use in the ritual game known as Tlachtlic, a cross between football and basketball. Its first practical use was credited to Joseph Priestly, the 18th century English theologian and philosopher best known for his discovery of oxygen, who noted that pencil marks could be "rubbed out" by the substance, and it has been known as rubber ever since.

Prior to 1839, the properties of rubber were dictated by weather conditions – malleable in hot weather and brittle in cold weather. Then Charles Goodyear discovered the process of vulcanization when a mixture of rubber, lead and sulfur were accidentally dropped onto a hot stove. This resulted in a product that was unaffected by weather and that came back to its original form if stretched. The process was soon refined; vulcanized rubber was resistant to water and chemical interactions and did not conduct electricity, making it suitable for a variety of products ranging from tires to raincoats.

Rubber trees required a hot, damp climate and were commonly found in the jungles of Southeast Asia. When the United States was cut off from virtually all of its sources of natural rubber during World War II, the production of synthetic rubber, which was relatively modest up until that time, increased precipitously. Synthetic rubber originated with two gases that were by-products of petroleum refining: butadiene and styrene. By mixing these gases in the presence of soapsuds in a reactor, the result was liquid latex. The dry rubber in this milky liquid was then coagulated into a solid form, washed, dried, and baled for shipment.[3]

By 2008, approximately 70 percent of all rubber was synthetic. Globally, rubber manufacturing had grown to become a $60 billion industry and its products contributed to almost every aspect of modern life – agriculture, transportation, aerospace, energy, and electronics, and health services.

While there was only one chemical type of natural rubber, there were roughly 20 different chemical types of synthetic rubber, and within each type there were many distinguishable grades. The different types and grades of rubber allowed manufacturers to choose the rubber that best met the demands of their customers.

Rubber can either be open cell or closed cell. In open cell rubber, the gas pockets connect with each other; an example would be a bath sponge, since water easily flows through the entire structure, displacing the air. In closed cell rubber, the gas forms discrete pockets, each completely surrounded by the solid material. An exercise mat would be an example of closed cell rubber, since the gas pockets are sealed from each other so that the mat cannot soak up water.

An open cell is analogous to Swiss cheese. Air can pass from one cell to another cell, much the same as a sponge. A closed cell, on the other hand, is analogous to a bunch of grapes. Each grape is a complete cell. If some are broken off, the others are still intact.

Monmouth's niche in the industry was as a leader in closed cell rubber manufacturing. A recognized leader in innovative technology, the company continually developed processes over the years to meet changing customer needs. Its rubber manufacturing equipment and processes kept the company competitive on a quality and cost level with manufacturers of similar closed cell sponge rubber and plastic foam products. All rubber manufacturing, lab testing, and office operations were housed at its 70 thousand square foot Long Branch location. The plant was 100 percent owned by John Bonforte.

All of its rubber was derived from petroleum and natural gas. Monmouth used domestic sources whenever possible. The oil and gas were refined at a refinery prior to coming to the factory.

Monmouth's state of the art production equipment included the following:

- Mixer- mixed together the formula ingredients.
- Mill- provided for the homogeneous blending of the rubber with a number of chemicals.
- Extruder- softened and pressurized the rubber.
- Press- formed the rubber into raw bales known as buns.
- Oven- cured (i.e., vulcanized) the rubber by blowing it to reduce it in weight to its desired density.

The mill, the extruder, and the press held their value the most and were difficult to replace. Moving them to another location would be very expensive given their weight and the possibility of damaging them. (See Exhibit 3 for a diagram of the process by which closed cell sponge rubber was made with these machines.)

Monmouth's factory workers could then use a machine called a skiver to split the buns into sheets or rolls that were then sold to various manufacturers and fabricators. (See Exhibit 4 for a diagram of Monmouth's role in the value chain for the rubber industry.)

Closed cell rubber clearly possessed many characteristics that allowed for the manufacture of many products that otherwise could not exist. One of these characteristics was shock absorption. Examples of some of the sports equipment that were made with closed cell rubber included helmets and pads for football and hockey. The closed cell rubber in these products insulated against cold and hot temperatures alike.

Exhibit 3. Monmouth Rubber & Plastics' Manufacturing Process

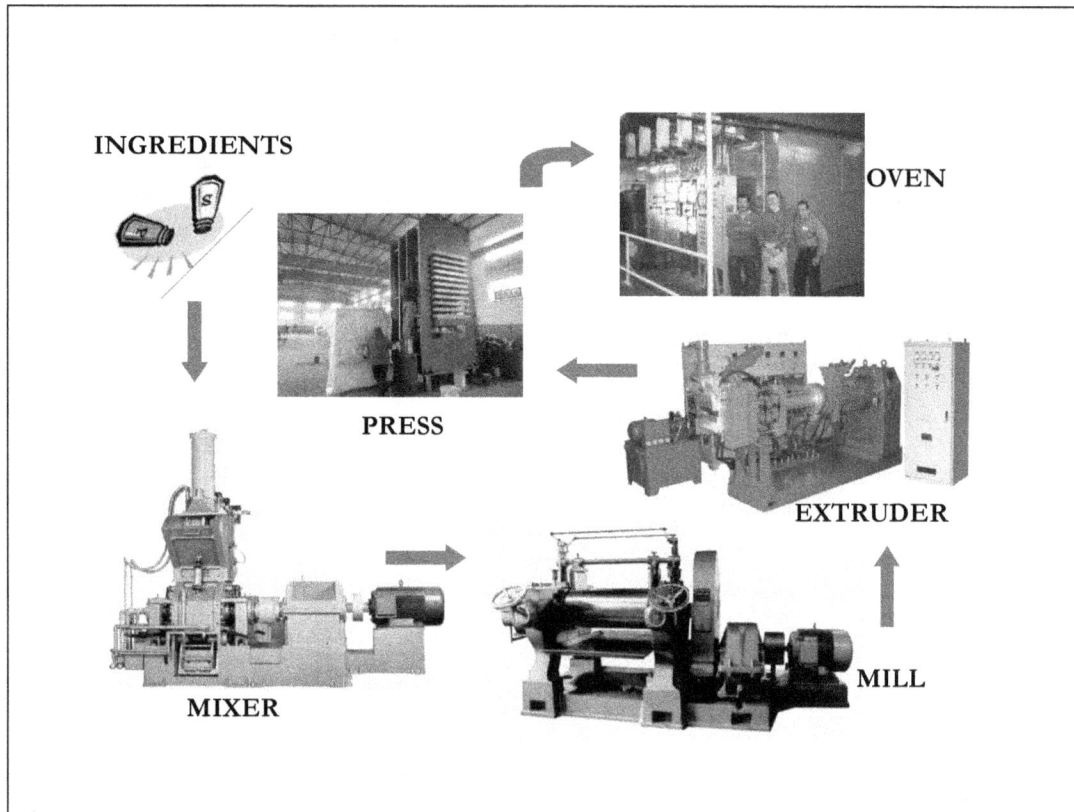

Source: Monmouth Rubber & Plastics

Exhibit 4. Monmouth Rubber & Plastics' Role in the Value Chain for the Rubber Industry

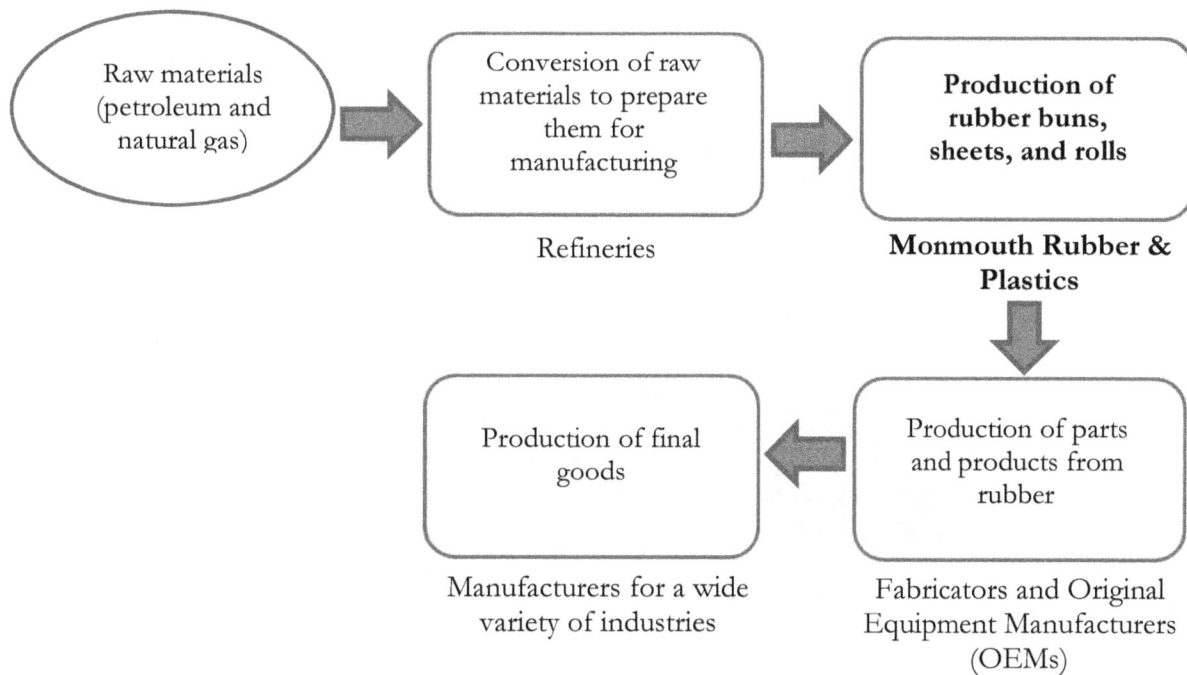

Rubberlite Inc., headquartered in Huntington, West Virginia, was one of the larger accounts that purchased closed cell rubber from Monmouth. Ed Littlehales, Rubberlite's purchasing manager, described the development of his firm's relationship with Monmouth:

> I've been at Rubberlite for a very long time. When I first came here, we were buying products from Monmouth. I thought the quality wasn't what it should have been. We moved on to some of its competitors for a number of years, but then those competitors started going out of business. We decided to give Monmouth another chance. They had moved away from trying to do everything and were just focused on making closed cell rubber. The fact that there are only a handful of closed cell bun manufacturers left in the U.S. today is a testament to Monmouth's success. John always does what he says he's going to do. He's got a family business, and that's what Rubberlite is too. That's one of the reasons why we like to do business with them. There's no bureaucracy. If I have a question, I go straight to John. His doors are always open.

Over the years, Monmouth became a recognized innovator of proprietary closed cell crosslinking technology and polymer blend technology[4], and the company was retained by a growing number of companies to assist with product development.

When outsourcing emerged as a common business strategy for U.S. manufacturers in the 1980s and the 1990s, Monmouth was one of the few manufacturers that completely resisted its pull. John Bonforte's operating philosophy had always been that U.S. manufacturing was the foundation of a strong economy. He demonstrated this philosophy with the following proclamation:

> When many expatriate manufacturers left the country and set up operations overseas in search of cheaper labor costs, subsidy offers, and the desire for better access to international markets, Monmouth Rubber & Plastics stayed loyal to the United States. To keep our factory on U.S. soil may appear to decrease our bottom line, but that type of thinking is short-sighted. You have to look at the big picture. At the end of the day, when our economy thrives, we thrive.

In 1996, Monmouth invested in excess of $1.5 million in equipment to ensure the quality of its product. "My priority was to increase the quality of our product," John would say, but a secondary benefit of the investment was that it increased Monmouth's quantity.

Before the end of the decade, John Jr. was working for the company. He was particularly instrumental in helping John strengthen the company's relationships with its customer base. As sales manager, John Jr. was heavily involved in setting strategies to facilitate the growth of the business.

In 2008, Monmouth achieved ISO certification. Going voluntarily through the International Organization for Standardization's certification process was a significant investment, but it was acknowledged as the gold standard for quality, which was very important for the business.

COMPETITION

Monmouth Rubber & Plastics' primary competitors were Rubatex Corporation, American National Rubber, and the Armacell Group.

Rubatex, a private company that had been John Bonforte's first employer, had its headquarters in Bedford, Virginia. Over the years, the company had suffered some setbacks. In 1995, it reached a settlement in a whistleblower lawsuit for a complaint that alleged it sold adhesives containing toluene, a chemical that was known to cause birth defects. In 2004, the company closed its doors for a short time, only to be saved when it was purchased by SEDO Chemical, a German manufacturer later that year. The company was then purchased on January 1, 2008 by Dominik Menakker, a German national, who became sole owner. The company remained an important competitor in the closed cell market due largely to its proprietary material Rubatex G231N.

American National Rubber, another private company, was headquartered in Ceredo, West Virginia and it employed about 60 people. This company was a serious competitor for Monmouth because of its reputation as the low cost provider among the manufacturers of closed cell rubber.

Armacell, a public company, had become the largest competitor in the industry following a managed buyout of Armstrong World Industries in 2000. This international company had manufacturing facilities in several countries. Its U.S. headquarters were in Mebane, North Carolina. In 2005, Armacell took over Monarch Rubber, whose plant in Spencer, West Virginia competed directly with Monmouth.

Among all the manufacturers in the rubber industry, these three companies posed serious challenges to Monmouth, whether it was due to the quality of their products, their competitive pricing, or their economies of scale.

As for how Monmouth competed with Armacell, a one-half billion dollar company, John recently said, "We think small," and added jokingly, "We look for their kneecap." Both John and John Jr. shared an aggressive stance toward other firms in the industry and they looked to exploit their competitors' weaknesses.

There were several rubber manufacturers overseas as well. John regarded the foreign manufacturers as serving a different market. The material produced overseas was mostly inferior to the material produced in the United States. As a result, the rubber that was manufactured in Japan, for example, was less costly than the rubber manufactured by American companies. John did not regard these manufacturers as direct competitors, notwithstanding the fact that a cheaper alternative could mount a threat especially in a difficult economy.

Monmouth Rubber & Plastics continued to survive in an industry that was constantly changing. It did this by recognizing the importance of finding new markets and the importance of investing in technology. These were two key competitive advantages at Monmouth.

A major obstacle materialized, however, which put in jeopardy its viability as a business – eminent domain.

EMINENT DOMAIN

Long Branch was a city of 30,000 residents on the Jersey shore. After its formation in 1867, it became a popular seaside resort. When President Garfield was shot in 1881, he asked to be brought to Long Branch to convalesce. Six other presidents – Ulysses S. Grant, Chester A. Arthur, Benjamin Harrison, Rutherford B. Hayes, William

McKinley, Theodore Roosevelt, and Woodrow Wilson – shared Garfield's love for Long Branch. Robert Louis Stevenson, Winslow Homer, and Buffalo Bill Cody were some of the public figures who made the city their summer retreat. (See Exhibit 5 for Long Branch's location on a New Jersey map.)

Exhibit 5. Long Branch, New Jersey

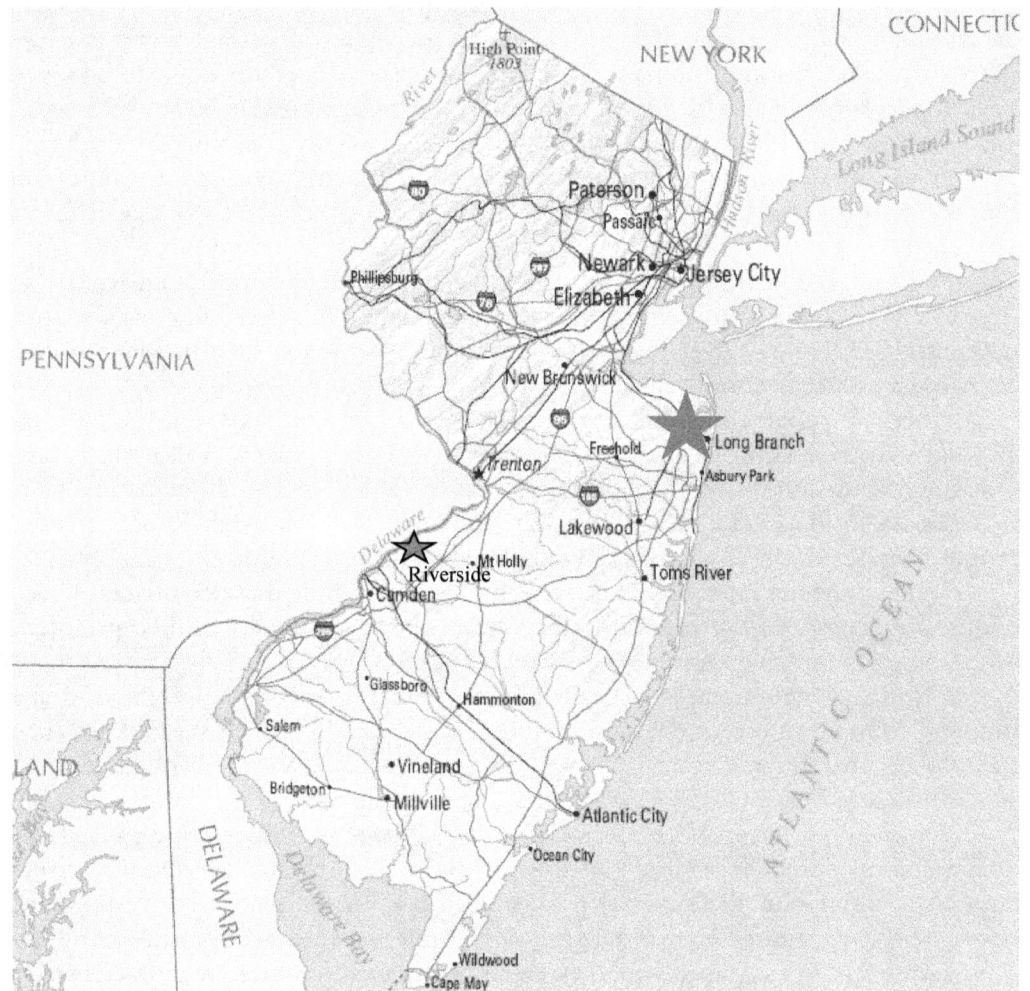

Source: www.citytowninfo.com

[*Note: Riverside, New Jersey, which is shown enlarged on the map, is 70 miles southwest of Long Branch.*]

When casino gambling was outlawed in the 1920s, the city lost its glamour as a seaside resort. It remained a regional tourist destination until 1987, when a fire broke out underneath the boardwalk in a utility box and destroyed the Long Branch pier. Several of the amusements along the pier as well as a water park were severely damaged, resulting in significant deterioration in waterfront properties. A series of storms over the years eroded the beach, further signaling the city's decline.

In 1996, the city reacted to the decline by establishing a redevelopment zone. An oceanfront master plan was drawn up to reverse the stagnation that had occurred and to revitalize the beach, the boardwalk, and the adjacent neighborhoods. (See Exhibit 6, next page, for a zoning map of the city of Long Branch showing the designated redevelopment zone, which indicates that Monmouth Rubber & Plastics was located within the redevelopment zone.[5]) As a consequence of the redevelopment plan, the city determined that it would invoke eminent domain – which had long been used by the government to justify seizing private land for public use to benefit the greater good – by identifying private homes and commercial properties within the redevelopment zone that were in need of improvement. In the 20th century, cities cleared properties for shopping malls and businesses to create jobs and revitalize the local economy. The redevelopment project in Long Branch was different because the city was prepared to seize and destroy properties in order to make room for new condominiums and town houses.

Exhibit 6. City of Long Branch Zoning Map (2007)

Source: City of Long Branch Office of Planning and Zoning.
[*Note: The Redevelopment Zone is shaded in yellow. The red star within the zone represents the location of Monmouth Rubber & Plastics.*]

Many of the property owners refused to sell regardless of what the city would pay, causing a public relations disaster for the mayor, Adam Schneider, as he tried to reclaim the glory days of Long Branch. Homeowners portrayed themselves as working class victims in the fight to replace their modest homes with more expensive homes. They argued that their homes were not blighted and that the city had decided that it no longer wanted them as residents.[6] They also stated that they had offered to spruce up the neighborhood to keep it from being leveled, but with the city asking them to sign disclaimers saying they might not be compensated for improvements if their property were later taken from them, any remodeling projects would be a waste of their money. Some of the homes had been in the same families for generations. Several homeowners were elderly and they felt they had nowhere else to go. (See Exhibit 7 for a photo from a 2007 article that appeared in *The New York Times* of a Long Branch resident in front of her parents' home who had been fighting the city for ten years to keep it from taking their home away.)

Exhibit 7. Long Branch Residents Protesting Eminent Domain

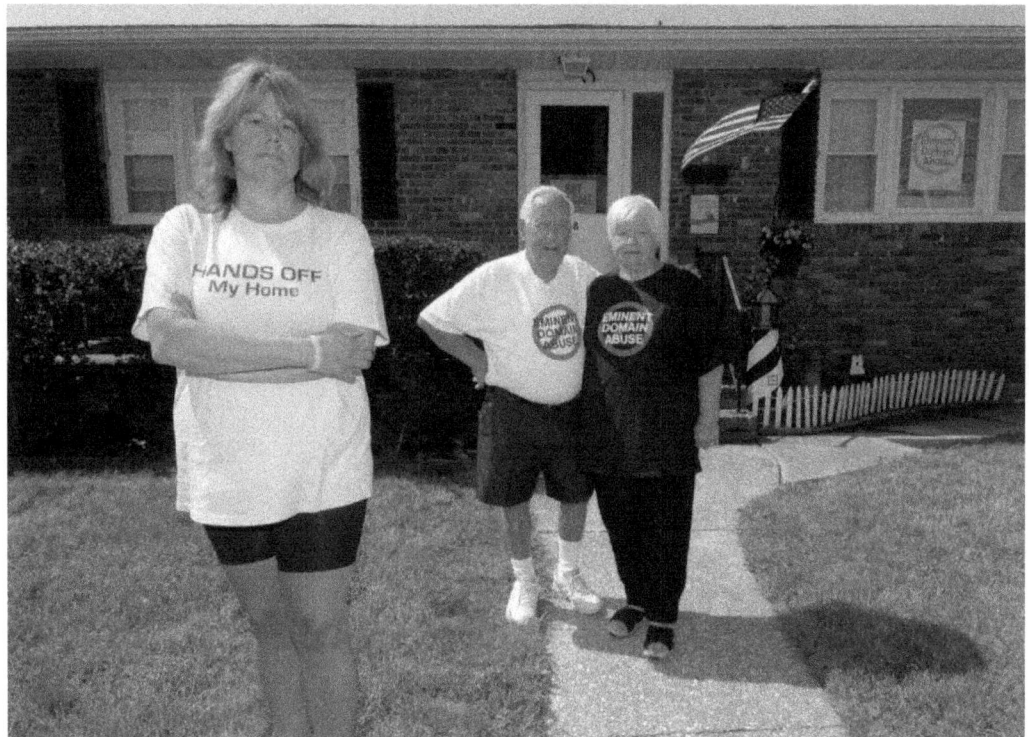

Source: Laura Pedrick/*The New York Times*/Redux, used with permission.

The homes at risk had been assessed in 2003 in the $200,000 range, while the new condos that were already being built adjacent to them were priced from $600,000 to $1.5 million. The new development was named Pier Village, and it opened in 2005 while the protests of eminent domain abuse continued. Around this time, the power of eminent domain was transferred to Matzel & Mumford, a subsidiary of K. Hovnanian, one of the largest property developers in the country. In other words, as John pointed out, "The protesters were not in a fight with the city, but rather with a private developer whose expected payoff would make it the real beneficiary of the new development – not the public."

In 2006, the Institute for Justice signed on as attorney for the property owners to appeal the case to the New Jersey Superior Court. The Institute for Justice, the nation's leading law firm on the issue of eminent domain abuse, had cemented its reputation when it successfully defended an Atlantic City homeowner after Donald Trump convinced a State agency to take her home so he could use the land for private limousine parking for his casino.

In September 2008, it was not clear to John when the court would issue a ruling or what the ruling would be.

THE RIVERSIDE FACILITY

Shortly after the news of the eminent domain declaration was announced, John realized that he needed to consider moving the business to a new location.[7] He traveled to the Southeastern United States and looked at different sites in Virginia, North Carolina, South Carolina, and Georgia. Sites in the South went for $18 per square foot. This compared favorably to the market price of $50-$60 per square foot at Monmouth's Long Branch facility.

John ultimately decided against moving the company to the South. He determined that most of his staff would not be able to relocate. Given that loyalty flowed both ways in his company – from the owners to the staff and from the staff to the owners – such a move would be far too disruptive and it would break an important bond that existed in the extended family of Monmouth Rubber & Plastics.

Instead, John found a building in South Jersey, in the town of Riverside, thirteen miles north of Camden along the Delaware River. In 2007, John bought the building, which was twice the size of the Long Branch building, for $17 per square foot.

The city of Camden, which had been a thriving industrialized city in the first half of the twentieth century, had been in economic decline for decades. As a direct result of its significant loss of manufacturing jobs, Camden's population also declined significantly. In 1999, its mayor declared bankruptcy for the city. Another consequence of the loss of jobs was a significant increase in the rate of crime, and Camden's reputation as one of the most dangerous cities in the United States. Although Long Branch had also been a city in decline in recent years, the employees at Monmouth were aware of the stigma that surrounded Camden. Moreover, they saw Long Branch as their home.

John didn't move Monmouth's operations to the new facility. He rented out some of the building for income, but the rest of the building remained vacant. He really didn't like the building. Aside from the fact that there still was a staff issue since it was an hour and a half drive from Long Branch, the building had an asbestos problem. It was a safety net for the business, however, as John negotiated with the developer in Long Branch.

RECESSION

An economic downturn commenced in late 2007 because of a global financial crisis and the U.S. subprime mortgage crisis. By 2008, economic growth in the United States had slowed down and unemployment was climbing. John noticed the effect on the stock market. "The Dow Jones Industrial Average was over 13,000 in May, and now in September it's dropped below 11,000," he said.

In this environment, businesses began to struggle to keep their heads above water. Other rubber manufacturers were closing down. Sales had generally grown at a steady pace at Monmouth Rubber & Plastics since 2000, and as a sign of this growth the company needed to increase its staff in the first half of 2008 by five employees. The company's resilience proved to be just as much a factor in its success as its marketing and investment skills, but given the bleak economic outlook for the foreseeable future the Bonfortes had reason for concern. (See Exhibit 8 for the trend in Monmouth's performance data.)

Exhibit 8. Performance Data for Monmouth Rubber & Plastics, 2000-2008

Year	Total Sales*	Employees
2000	$3,000,000	34
2001	$3,200,000	34
2002	$3,500,000	35
2003	$3,400,000	35
2004	$4,800,000	35
2005	$5,200,000	36
2006	$5,100,000	36
2007	$4,800,000	37
2008**	$3,000,000	42

Source: Monmouth Rubber and Plastics
[*Notes: * Earnings were roughly 20 percent of total sales. ** 2008 sales reflect data for the first six months of the year.*]

THE OFFER

John had received three other offers for the business over the prior twelve months. He hadn't really considered any of them. He was not actively selling, but some firms had shown interest because Monmouth Rubber & Plastics was a well-run company that continued to perform well. The offer of $5.5 million that John had received the day before was substantially higher than the previous ones.

The offer was for the business and the equipment. It was independent of the real estate, which was debt-free and worth approximately $1.5 million to $2 million. Without a manufacturing facility, John knew that the buyer would have to stay in Long Branch. The buyer expressed an interest in taking out a long term lease with an option to buy the property.

The offer came from a strategic buyer who was in manufacturing, but was not a direct competitor. The buyer was looking to expand its market. John found this type of buyer to be preferable to a financial buyer, which was typically a private equity firm.

John was also attracted to the fact that the buyer was a family business. The owner had toured Monmouth's facility prior to making the offer and John liked him. The owner told John that he wouldn't lay anyone off.

THE DILEMMA

John Jr. placed his coffee cup back down on the table. "So you're really considering the offer?"

"I am," John replied confidently. "Any offer that's five times earnings is a good offer. If you couple that with the fact that the value of the business has been compromised because of the threat of eminent domain, smart money says we should cash out and maybe I can retire."

John Jr. said, "He might have to move the business sooner than he likes if the city invokes eminent domain."

"That's why we got Riverside, son," John replied.

"Well, how do we know for sure that he'll take care of everyone?" John Jr. asked.

"Listen to me. The offer is very good. Maybe I can tell him I'll consider something less if he puts certain guarantees in writing. If the business has to relocate, I want everyone who makes the move to get an appropriate monetary incentive. For anyone who can't make the move, I want them to get an appropriate severance package. Including those terms in a contract is important to me." He smiled assuringly at John Jr. and said, "I love our company."

"I love it, too, Dad," he said, smiling back at his father. "You know that we've talked about the possibility of me taking over the company. Well, I'm ready. I'm sure there's a way for us to keep the business in the family. Let's explore different ways to ensure a comfortable retirement for you while I build up my equity in the company."

John cleared his throat. "I don't know, Junior. My heart says yes but my head is telling me no. I know that you're interested, but I'm concerned about the business. I don't know how the eminent domain is going to turn out. I don't know if I want you to have to shoulder the problems that we are facing. We might not get another offer like this. You would be able to do a lot of things with the proceeds of the sale." He got up from his seat and walked over to the other side of the table, placing his hand firmly on his son's shoulder. "Come on, let's leave. I don't have to get back to the buyer for another few days.

Notes

[1] The names of the grandchildren as well as two other individuals in the case have been disguised.

[2] The value added manager developed enhancements for the company's products to help differentiate them from those offered by competitors.

[3] The key distinction between natural and synthetic rubber is the source for the rubber (i.e., tapped from tropical and subtropical trees vs. refined from petroleum and natural gas). After that, the manufacturing process is essentially the same, with the blending of various chemicals to enhance the properties of the rubber, forming the rubber, and heating it.

[4] A polymer is a generic chemical name for all synthetic rubber and plastic materials. Three well known families of polymers are the styrenic family (polystyrene as a plastic and styrene butadiene rubber, or SBR, as a rubber); the polyolefin family (polyethylene as a plastic and ethylene propylene diene monomer, or EPDM, as a rubber); and the vinyl nitrile family (poly vinyl chloride, or PVC, as a plastic). Rubber and plastic within the same family are chemically compatible and therefore can be crosslinked to form a covalent bond. Products

with a high plastic content range from lawn furniture to Tupperware bowls. These products are lightweight, tough, inexpensive, do not stretch, and cannot withstand high temperatures. Products with a high rubber content range from automobile tires to baby bottle nipples and rubber bands. These products can be stretched but are able to hold their shape after they are formed (even at high temperatures).

[5] A number of Monmouth Rubber & Plastics' employees also lived within the redevelopment zone.

[6] Urban blight is the deterioration that causes previously functioning cities to experience a decrease in jobs and infrastructure, changing population, and an increase in crime. One of the policies that local governments have utilized to reverse blight is eminent domain.

[7] John also sold off a number of small investment properties that he owned in the Long Branch area during this time.

Houston We Have A Problem: They Paid Themselves Bonuses!

NACRA
NORTH AMERICAN CASE
RESEARCH ASSOCIATION

Pascale Lapointe-Antunes, Brock University

Deborah McPhee, Brock University

Amanda Walsh's first year as Vanderville Plastics Company's (VPC) controller had been quite tumultuous. She had discovered on her first day on the job that VPC's financial situation was precarious, and had since witnessed a change in ownership, repeated requests for funding to the new owners to help alleviate VPC's severe cash flow issues, and more recently, the sudden resignation of Peter Giroux, the company's Chief Financial Officer (CFO). As a result of Giroux's resignation, Amanda was now acting interim CFO and reported directly to Michael Stratton, the Chief Executive Officer (CEO).

A consultant had been hired by the new owners to better understand the causes of VPC's cash flow shortages, and he never seemed satisfied with Amanda's answers. Michael wanted the consultant to make all of his requests to Amanda through him. However, Amanda had no choice but to answer one of the owners' questions when he called her to enquire about a $1 million decrease in accrued liabilities in January 2006. Amanda discovered to her great disbelief that the new owners did not know about the recent payout of bonuses for the 2005 financial year.

Scared and angry, Amanda started to think about the succession of events since she came to VPC to better understand what this all meant, what was likely to happen next, and what she should do.

VANDERVILLE PLASTICS COMPANY

VPC, a plastics injection molding company, was founded in 1962 by the Vanderville family. A major player in the plastics industry, they supplied products to original equipment manufacturers (OEM) in the health care industry. The Canadian plastics industry was a sophisticated, multi-faceted sector encompassing plastic products manufacturing, machinery, molds, and resins. The plastics industry was very fragmented. There were many hundreds of small and medium enterprises (SMEs), and about a dozen large firms (500+ employees) operating domestically. It was estimated that about 95 percent of this sector was Canadian-owned. The industry was concentrated in Ontario, Quebec, British Columbia and Alberta. VPC was located in Meadowbrook, a small borough close to Vancouver, British Columbia, Canada. VPC's location was strategically selected to be near an area heavily populated by hospitals.

The Vandervilles had planned to pass on their company to their two children, but the latter made it clear they wanted to pursue other opportunities. Private equity firms were very interested in working with firms in the plastics industry to earn a lucrative return because plastics manufacturing had grown faster than the general economy, and twice as fast as other manufacturing businesses over the past decade. Globally, plastics was also thought of as one of the industries that would drive innovation, technology, and the knowledge jobs of the future. As word spread that the Vandervilles were looking to sell, VPC quickly became an attractive target for private equity investors. A Miami based private equity firm (Miami) acquired VPC in 1996 for $20 million and sold 20% of VPC's common shares to some of the senior employees (see Exhibit 1).

Miami planned on buying out several smaller companies to leverage the relationships that VPC had already established with high profile multinationals. They kept the company name because the Vanderville family was highly respected in the industry. Between 1996 and 1998, VPC acquired one company from New York City (New York) that continued to operate independently, and two companies from British Columbia that were amalgamated into VPC (Meadowbrook) (see Exhibit 1). Meadowbrook handled the administration, tax planning, and strategic planning for both locations.

By 2005, VPC had grown to 400 employees in Canada, and 120 employees in New York City. The organizational structure included a Board of Directors made up of the equity owners, the Chief Executive Officer (CEO), Michael Stratton, and the Chief Financial Officer (CFO), Peter Giroux, CPA, CA. There was no separate audit committee. Peter Giroux and Michael Stratton reported directly to Miami. The Vice Presidents of Manufacturing, Commercial Services, Sales, and Engineering (the VPs) reported directly to Michael and were one level below Peter. The Human Resources (HR) Director was on the level below the VPs, and the Controller another level below. In turn, each VP had managers and supervisors with staff reporting to each of their positions. New York's General Manager (GM), Brent Wiseman, reported to Michael (see Exhibit 2 for the organizational chart).

AMANDA WALSH

Amanda Walsh graduated from Simon Fraser University's business school with a concentration in accounting in 1998 before pursuing a Certified Management Accountant (CMA) designation[1]. Amanda had been employed by a major electronics supplier as an Assistant Controller for five years when she started to feel that she was no longer challenged. She applied for the position of Controller at VPC in November 2004. It was a smaller organization that suited her desire to be more involved with day-to-day operations and major decision making.

Amanda was interviewed by VPC's HR Director, Janis Turner, Peter, and Michael in early December. After the interview, she was even more excited about the prospects of joining VPC. She could be working for someone who could teach her a lot and doing some interesting and challenging things. It was exactly what she wanted. She received her letter of employment offer at the end of December 2004. VPC paid salaries between the 75th and 90th percentile for the industry. Bonuses were paid if VPC met the performance targets established by its owners. Amanda's bonus could range between 10% and 15% of her salary. She resigned from her position with her previous employer in January 2005 and began her employment with VPC in February 2005.

AMANDA'S RUDE AWAKENING

On February 7th of 2005, her first day at VPC, Peter introduced Amanda to her team - a senior financial analyst, a financial analyst, an accounts receivable coordinator and an accounts payable coordinator (see Exhibit 2). Peter remained evasive when she asked for the latest financial statements and told her to spend some time learning about VPC by meeting with the senior financial analyst instead. After a week of avoiding her requests, Peter finally provided Amanda with the management letter prepared by VPC's auditors, a large international accounting firm, for the year ended November 30, 2003. The letter was dated September 30, 2004. It included an overview of the audit, a discussion of significant accounting, financial reporting and auditing matters, recommendations for improvements in internal controls, a summary of unadjusted differences (SUD), and consolidated financial statements.

To her disbelief, Amanda discovered that the financial statements for the years ended November 30, 2002 and 2003 were still draft (see Exhibit 3). The balance sheets looked terrible, VPC was incurring large losses, and the following note was printed on the title page:

> The Company's current banking agreements have now expired. The Company is currently in negotiations between management and the Company's banking syndicate regarding the establishment of new credit facilities and covenants. As a result, the Company's ability to continue as a going concern and to pay down existing credit facilities is dependent on generating adequate cash flows from operations over the upcoming year, and the continued financial support of its shareholders and creditors. Depending on the final resolution of these matters, the financial statement presentation and related disclosure in the notes to the financial statements for the long-term debt and financing costs will be modified to reflect the circumstances noted. Should the financial statements require release prior to this date, then significant adjustments to the financial statements would be required, to disclose these going concern assumptions and the possibility that the going concern basis may not be appropriate; for example if repayment were to be demanded for the existing credit facilities. This disclosure is currently not reflected in this draft of the financial statements." [2]

"Possibly *not* a going concern?!" When Amanda said those words out loud, they did not sound real. "How can I have so many responsibilities for the financial operations of this company and not even know the auditors think VPC might not be a going concern?" Amanda was angry and hurt...and, she felt betrayed. Neither Peter nor Michael had mentioned such significant issues at any point during her interview. Amanda immediately went to Peter to ask him why.

Peter told her they didn't want her to decline their offer because of it. He asked her to please not worry, that he could clarify what was going on, and that everything would be fine. He went on to explain that when Miami acquired VPC in 1996, the Canadian dollar was trading in the mid- to high 1.30s to the US dollar, eventually reaching the low 1.60s for a good part of 2001 and 2002. The strong US dollar gave Canadian companies in labour intensive industries a major competitive advantage over their US competitors because it kept their labour costs much lower, and their margins high. This was reflected in the multiple of earnings before interest, taxes and depreciation (EBITDA) VPC had to pay for the three companies acquired in the late 90's. Miami had worked with a syndicate of well-known banks to fund the purchases, leaving VPC with $30 million US debt. Exhibit 1 shows the ownership structure.

In 2003, the Canadian dollar appreciated dramatically, reaching the high 1.20s by the end of the year, and pretty much everyone in the industry suffered significant setbacks. VPC got to the point where they couldn't service the debt anymore. The banks allowed VPC to operate under forbearances for a while, but soon enough the company had to start trading off preferred equity in exchange for some of the debt. The original banks eventually sold their debt and preferred equity at a discount to two other private equity firms from Texas (Houston) and New Jersey (Jersey) (see Exhibit 1). Houston, Jersey and Miami agreed VPC should take advantage of the debt transfer that had happened to clean up its balance sheet before finalizing the 2003 audit. The audit would be done retroactively so VPC could avoid the going concern note and secure third-party financing, and Miami contain its losses.

VPC's financial statements were prepared in accordance with US generally accepted accounting principles (GAAP) to satisfy the needs of its American owners. Peter was not able to complete the debt restructuring because Houston and Jersey needed to agree on new payment terms for the restructuring to comply with SFAS 15.[3] According to Peter, Houston was great to work with, but Jersey was more difficult and not very supportive. They were confrontational, particularly with their co-investors from Houston. To complicate matters further, Miami was seeking an exit strategy, and talks were underway on this initiative. Peter told Amanda he still hoped to have everything finalized by the end of 2005.

Amanda left Peter's office still perplexed about VPC's financial position and why Miami was seeking to exit. Amanda realized she had no choice but to stick with VPC for now. Reputation was important, and she did not want anybody to think she was a quitter. Plastics was still a great industry, and she would definitely be challenged. Her job was just going to be more difficult than she had thought.

AMANDA SETTLES IN

Amanda did not regret her decision as she settled into her new position. Her direct reports were qualified and pleasant. Peter was present and involved, and he was always available to answer her questions or concerns. She was learning a lot.

Peter kept Amanda's interactions with the VPs and Michael to a minimum. Peter and Michael tightly controlled the flow of information within and outside of VPC. Most of the corporate governance documentation, such as the shareholders' agreement, were not made available to Amanda. Few of the internal controls were documented, and the job descriptions were not current. The organization chart had not been updated in years. Amanda watched cautiously every month when representatives from Miami, Houston and Jersey came to town and met with Michael and Peter for board meetings. The VPs of Sales, Commercial Services, Manufacturing and Engineering sometimes joined them for parts of the meetings.

Peter also maintained complete control over HR and payroll. Amanda was perplexed about the apparent lack of HR integration. Both Dora Parsons, the payroll manager, and Janis reported to Peter. Dora submitted the payroll to BER, the external payroll service. She made changes for wage rates, new hires, terminations, reviewed BER's payments for accuracy, and she examined BER's report of changes made in the period. The auditors had raised concerns over a lack of segregation of payroll duties in their report to the audit committee. They thought management should review payroll prior to payment, examine BER's report of changes, and review the overall payments made for reasonableness. Janis was a designated Certified Human Resources Professional (CHRP), and Amanda knew she was sometimes frustrated with not being at the table with the senior members of the organization. One day as Peter and Michael were meeting with the board, Janis told Amanda she wished VPC made better use of her expertise. She was not involved with the design of the bonus structure when it was developed and was not privy to any of the information on bonuses. Janis had tried to discuss her concerns with Peter and Michael, but Peter made it clear that it was not her place to be involved. Michael kept putting off reviewing the reporting relationships, saying he needed to think about it. Amanda's previous organization had a lot more involvement from HR, and there was a VP of Human Resources. She wondered why none of the recommended changes from the auditors had been made.

Miami evaluated Meadowbrook's performance based on its ability to meet the non-consolidated adjusted EBITDA target established at the beginning of each year as part of the budgeting process. Adjusted EBITDA excluded management fees, as well as one-time costs and unusual expenses that were at the discretion of the owners. Bonuses were earned if the target was met. The overall bonus pool in $ was decided by Michael, Peter and the Miami owners at the beginning of the year. Maximum individual earned bonuses as percentage of total salary depended on rank, and included both a guaranteed component tied to meeting the adjusted EBITDA target and a discretionary component allocated by Michael and Peter as outlined in Table 1:

Table 1 - Maximum Bonus as Percentage of Total Salary			
Rank	Guaranteed bonus as % of total salary	Discretionary bonus as % of total salary	Maximum bonus as % of total salary
CEO and CFO	37.5%	12.5%	50.0%
Vice-Presidents	30.0%	10.0%	40.0%
HR Director and Controller	10.0%	5.0%	15.0%
Sales representatives	15.0%	5.0%	20.0%
Supervisory employees	7.5%	2.5%	10.0%

Declared bonuses were supposed to be paid after the audit of the financial statements was completed to assure management did not artificially inflate EBIDTA. These financial reporting requirements had not been made part of the corporate governance documents. The bonuses were paid before the audit was completed for the years ended November 30, 2003 and 2004 because the recent delays in issuing audited financial statements were caused by Houston and Jersey and considered to be outside of management's control. Bonuses for the year ended November 30, 2004 were declared and paid in early 2005 based on the draft non-consolidated financial statements prepared by Amanda's predecessor. Peter asked Amanda to make the finalization of the 2004 financial statements and the preparation of the corporate tax return a priority when she was hired. Amanda, who was much more acquainted with Canadian GAAP, saw this as an opportunity to become more familiar with US GAAP and perfect her understanding of VPC's business. She was done by the end of May 2005, in time to file VPC's corporate tax return before the Canadian Revenue Agency's (CRA) deadline.

Just like Peter had said, VPC's debt was not indicative of the company's success, it was just an anchor weighing it down. The Canadian operation was doing well from an

EBITDA perspective. It just couldn't service its debt and the legacy interest was hurting its cash flow. The cash flow issues started to balloon out of control in the fall of 2005. The estimated cash shortfall to the end of the year was over $3 million. VPC's days payable outstanding (DPO) was over 110 days, more than 70 days longer than industry, and vendors were threatening to stop supplying them. The company would not be able to meet payroll if it paid its suppliers. Equity owners were the only available source of funding until the restructuring was completed, and there had been no progress made on that front.

Miami sold all of their $20 million investment in VPC's equity to Houston and Jersey for half a million dollars, pennies for the dollar, in October of 2005 (see Exhibit 1). The common stock was not worth anything because of the large amount of debt on the books (see Exhibit 3). The two private equity firms already controlled the debt. They now also owned about 80 percent of the equity too, with the balance being held by current and former employees. The first order of business for Michael and Peter was to get an influx of cash. VPC's technicians were highly skilled and the industry was suffering from a shortage of qualified labor. If any of them left as a result of missing payroll, they would easily be able to find work at a competitor, and it would be very difficult for VPC to replace them. VPC needed $1.6 million to repay one of their largest suppliers, $1 million to repay other vendors, and $400,000 as extra working capital. Houston stepped up and loaned $3 million at very high interest rates in late November 2005. Jersey was not pleased with this move by Houston and refused to lend.

BONUSES ARE PAID

Amanda kept busy finalizing the Canadian operation's non-consolidated financial statements for the year ended November 30, 2005 (see Exhibit 4 for an extract) while Peter was dealing with the new owners. She met with Peter in mid-December 2005 to go over the preliminary financial statements.

Amanda told Peter she was done with the 2005 non-consolidated financial statements, except for a couple of outstanding accruals he needed to approve before she booked them. The first one was for expected losses on work-in-process. According to the cost estimates provided by the VP- Manufacturing, expected losses of $725,000 needed to be recognized for the year ended November 30, 2005.[4] The second one was for $225,000 in development costs that were capitalized in early 2005 because VPC expected to be able to bill them back to one of their customers as design costs. The purchase order for which the prototype had been built had not yet materialized from the customer.

Peter thanked Amanda for her diligence and hard work. He asked her to leave the preliminary statements and accruals with him, so he could finalize everything before the Christmas break and work on the board package for the January 17, 2006 meeting.

Peter said he was not sure whether he would book the expected losses on work-in-process now or wait until the contracts to which they relate were completed and the actual losses known. There had been no progress on the restructuring, so the financial statements wouldn't be audited until then. He also said he would probably wait to expense the capitalized development costs until it was more certain the purchase order would not come.

Amanda did not hear further from Peter about the financial statements and she did not ask. She took advantage of the 10-day Christmas break to rest and spend time with her family.

On January 5, 2006, the third day of work after the Christmas break, total bonuses of $900,000 were declared for the year ended November 30, 2005. Every employee received a letter signed by Michael informing them the Canadian operation had exceeded its adjusted EBITDA target of $3 million for the year ended November 30, 2005 and telling them the amount and breakdown of their bonus. Individual bonuses are summarized in the table below:

Table 2 – 2005 Bonus Allocation		
	Bonus in $ (individual)	Bonus in $ (total for the rank)
Michael Stratton	$105,000	$105,000
Peter Giroux	$100,000	$100,000
Vice-Presidents	$ 75,000	$300,000
Janis Turner and Amanda Walsh	$ 12,500	$ 25,000
Sales representatives	$ 20,000	$180,000
Supervisory employees	$ 10,000	$100,000
Non-management employees	$500 to $1,000	$ 90,000
Total		**$900,000**

Amanda was awarded a 15% bonus in the amount of $12,500. Peter told her she earned her full discretionary bonus because she had done a great job amidst the organization's strife and reached all her goals. He indicated it was important for the owners to reward the employees for their efforts. He also told Amanda that Dora, the payroll manager would be taking care of the bonus accrual. Amanda's thoughts immediately went to Janis, wondering what she was thinking of all this. She knew that Janis would probably be upset because she would not have been privy to any of the discussion on bonus allocation and the payouts through payroll.

The bonuses were paid on January 28, 2006. Amanda knew Meadowbrook was making its target but with the equity debt accumulating, she was astonished that the bonuses were being paid out so early. There was surely enough cash to pay out the bonuses with the influx of cash from Houston. Still, she had not expected anything before at least the summer given the financial position of VPC.

THE NEW OWNERS GET INVOLVED

In February of 2006, Michael Stratton went back to the owners and asked for another $2 million in working capital funding. Although the previous investment had helped calm down some suppliers, there were still more than $1.5 million in payables over 60 days and VPC was afraid of missing payroll again. Peter asked Amanda to prepare detailed reports on VPC's working capital cycle, including its days sales outstanding (DSO), DPO, order backlog, customer deposits, and shipments calendar to support the request. Jersey still refused to provide funding, and Houston seemed to have a hard time understanding the reasons for this new request for cash despite the support provided by Peter. The income statement was showing positive EBITDA, there were no capital expenditures, and the interest payments had been reduced, so it just did not make any sense to them that VPC needed cash again. They asked for an EBITDA to cash reconciliation from November to February to understand how to account for the difference (see Exhibit 5).

Houston eventually agreed to inject the funds, at the same high interest rate, but decided to bring in a consultant, Robert Black, to investigate further and be in a better position to evaluate VPC's future cash needs. Robert was sent to Meadowbrook for as long as would be needed with the official mandate of "helping management improve its accountability and better communicate with the owners".

By April 2006, Amanda felt something was not right with Peter. He wasn't arriving at work as early as he had in the past, was going out for long lunches, and was leaving early. There were a lot of closed-door meetings between Peter and Robert. Robert wanted more detailed reconciliations to support the $4 million change in working capital accounts between November and February. He was particularly interested in the change in accrued liabilities. Peter insisted the accrued liabilities balance did not mean anything because it included significant legacy interest and foreign exchange translation losses that would be written-off once the pending capital restructuring was completed. This did not seem to satisfy Robert. He wanted to see reconciliations, pro forma financial statements, and cash flow forecasts stripped out of the foreign exchange effects and legacy debt and interest. Peter was passing back the consultant's requests to Amanda. She was a bit lost because she knew that Peter could answer his questions much more quickly then she could. Peter told her this was a good way to grow and that he knew she could handle it. But Robert never seemed satisfied with the information provided to him, even if it was exactly what he had asked for.

AMANDA WALSH, CFO

Peter Giroux resigned as CFO from VPC in late May 2006. He came and told Amanda he had decided to leave because he was tired of having to deal with Houston's and Jersey's constant questioning. It was time for him to move on.

Michael Stratton called Amanda. He asked her if she could step in as interim CFO for six months. He was okay with starting the recruiting process for a new CFO if she didn't feel up to it but was really hoping she would give the position a try.

Amanda could not believe that this was happening. She had been dreaming of the day she would become a CFO, and now that it finally materialized, she was being asked to step up to be… the Captain of the Titanic! She had a long conversation with her husband. If things went well, she had the opportunity to play a key role in rebuilding VPC. But what if they didn't? She came to realize she could always move on. So she accepted the position and began hiring some co-op students to help her out.

It didn't take long for Amanda to find herself in the thick of things. With Peter no longer there, Robert was coming to her to get answers to his inexhaustible questions. He just couldn't understand why VPC constantly needed more working capital funding when the income statement showed positive EBITDA. He asked for a detailed monthly cash flow analysis from August 2005 to today, showing exactly why the funding provided by Houston was needed and how it was used. He wanted the name of the suppliers, the invoice numbers, the dates, everything.

Amanda, who was already busy enough, wondered who Robert thought he was. She reported to Michael, not to him. Amanda went to Michael and told him she was feeling a bit overwhelmed with Robert's constant requests. She told him she felt as if she was providing him with the same information over and over again, and that she was not sure what he was after exactly. Michael told Amanda he was starting to feel frustrated too, and that he knew Robert was not the most accommodating guy around. He said he would ask Robert to stop going to Amanda directly and make his requests through him first. But he wanted her to provide him with what he needed and to be as transparent as possible.

Amanda left feeling she had done the right thing. She had a lot of respect for Michael. He had started on the shop floor and progressed through the ranks until he became the CEO. He was hands-on, and very good at managing sales and relationships. He just needed a strong financial person by his side. Amanda felt that since she had only been there a little more than a year it made sense for Robert to speak directly to Michael. She was relieved she could count on him.

KEN'S CALL

A couple of weeks later, Amanda's phone started ringing. She glanced at the call display screen before picking up: it was Ken Duffy, one of Houston's principals. Why in the world was one of the owners calling her directly? She took a deep breath and answered the phone.

Ken told Amanda he was happy to finally chat with her. He said Houston didn't really know much about her until recently. He knew they were asking for a lot and that things were really hard, and he wanted to offer some support. He promised it would be worth her while for her to stick it out.

Amanda took a moment to calm herself down before telling Ken she was happy to chat with him too. She told him she was shocked when she saw the financial statements during her first week at VPC and just about left right then, but that she was happy she stuck it out because she had learned a lot even if it had been rough. She also said she really appreciated his vote of confidence.

As the conversation went on, Ken began asking for more information. He told her Peter had not been very forthcoming with Robert, never really answering some of their questions. He knew Robert was asking for a lot from her, but they needed to understand why the accrued liabilities had dropped by close to $1 million at the end of January 2006. He didn't want to hear it was because of the legacy interest or foreign exchange translation gains because no progress had been made on the restructuring. He said the funding Houston had provided in November 2005 was supposed to be used to settle $2.6 million in accounts payable, not other accrued liabilities. So, could she please explain to him what had happened.

Of course, she could! Amanda told him it was the incentive payment - $900,000 in bonuses were accrued on January 5, 2006 and paid out on January 28, 2006. Ken interrupted. He asked what bonuses she was talking about. He said Houston had never agreed on a bonus plan for 2005, that it had never even been discussed.

There was a long lull of silence. Amanda felt ill when she realized what the concern had been all along – it was the bonuses.

Amanda went on to explain they were indeed the 2005 bonuses, declared in early January based on meeting the $3M adjusted EBITDA target for the year. She told Ken that Peter had said the owners wanted to reward the employees for their efforts. She also told him the payroll manager was the one who had booked the accrual and managed the payout. She asked if he wanted her to speak to Dora to see if she had any supporting documentation she could provide to him. But Ken wanted to speak to his partners first. He told Amanda he would get back to her shortly.

Amanda stared at her phone in disbelief. They didn't know! Scared and angry, she started to think about the succession of events since she came to VPC to better understand what this all meant, what was likely to happen next, and what she should do.

Exhibit 1: Changes in Ownership

1962 to 1996

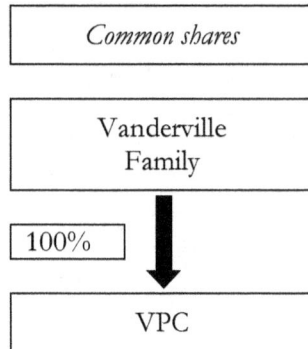

1996

Miami purchases VPC and sells 20% of the common shares to a group of senior employees.

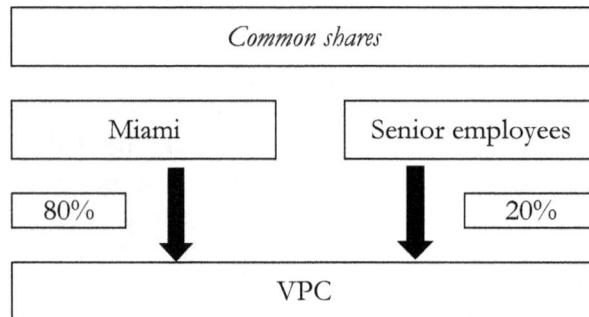

1998

VPC contracts $US 30M in debt to finance the purchase 3 companies.

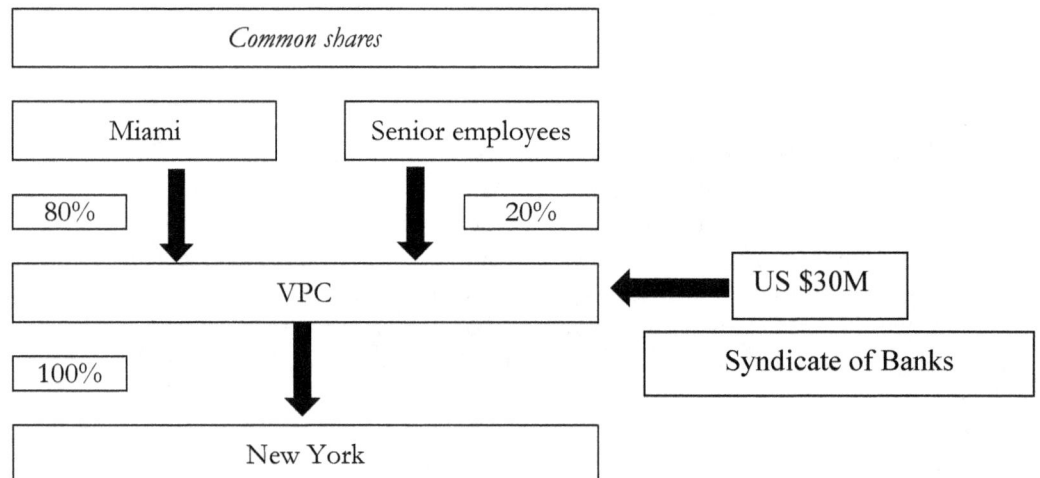

2003 to 2005

VPC starts to trade off preferred equity in exchange for some of its debt. The syndicate of banks sells their debt and preferred equity at a discount to Houston and Jersey.

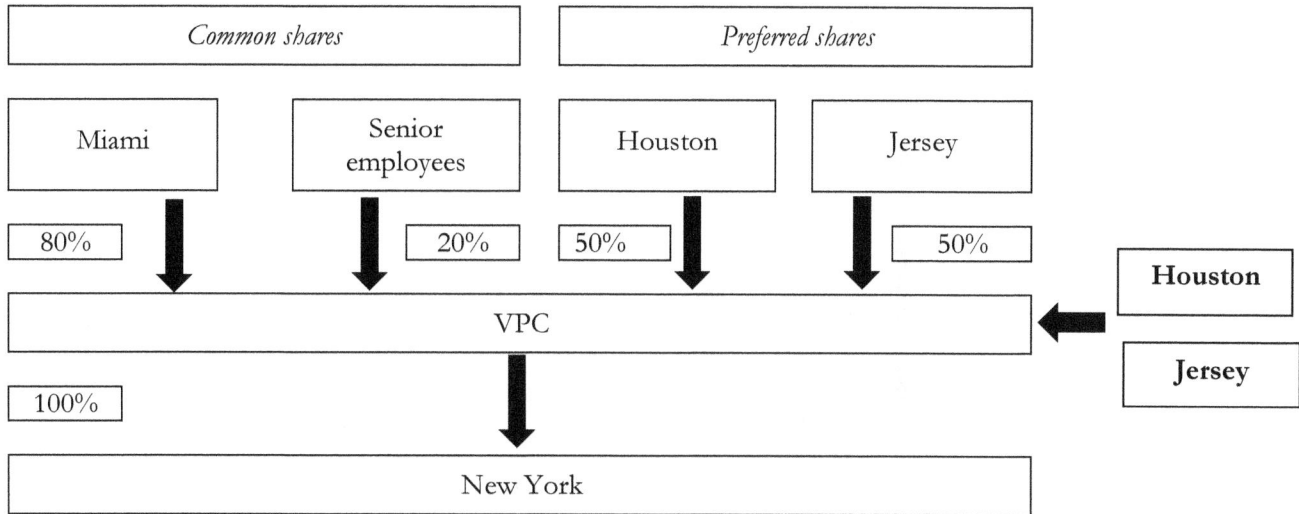

Common shares		Preferred shares	
Miami	Senior employees	Houston	Jersey
80%	20%	50%	50%

VPC ◀ Houston / Jersey

100%

New York

2005-2006

Miami sells its common shares to Houston and Jersey.

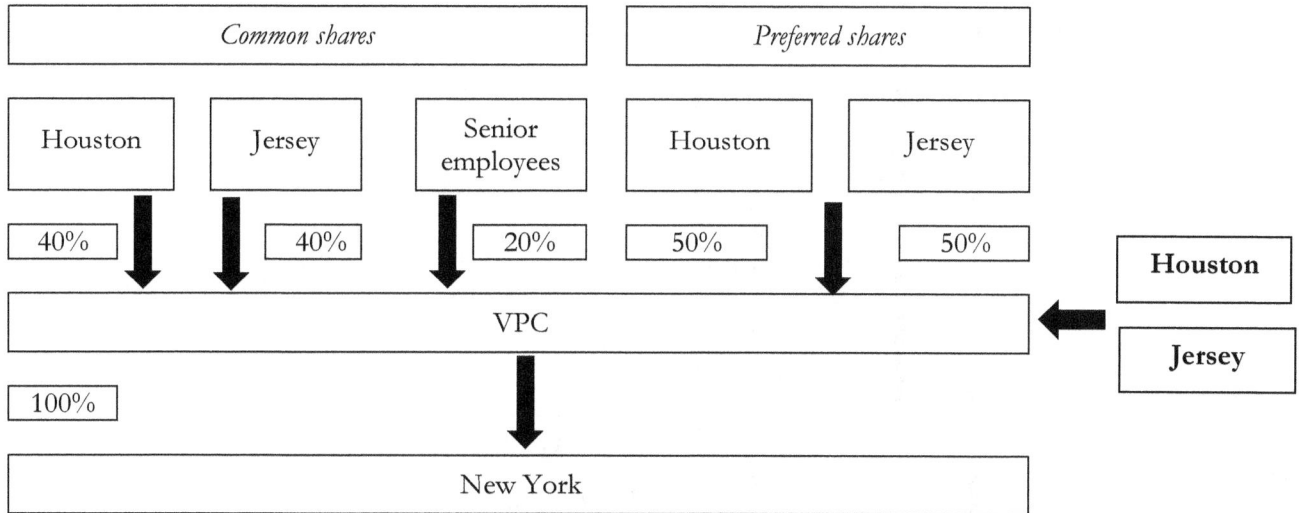

Common shares			Preferred shares	
Houston	Jersey	Senior employees	Houston	Jersey
40%	40%	20%	50%	50%

VPC ◀ Houston / Jersey

100%

New York

Exhibit 2: Organizational Chart

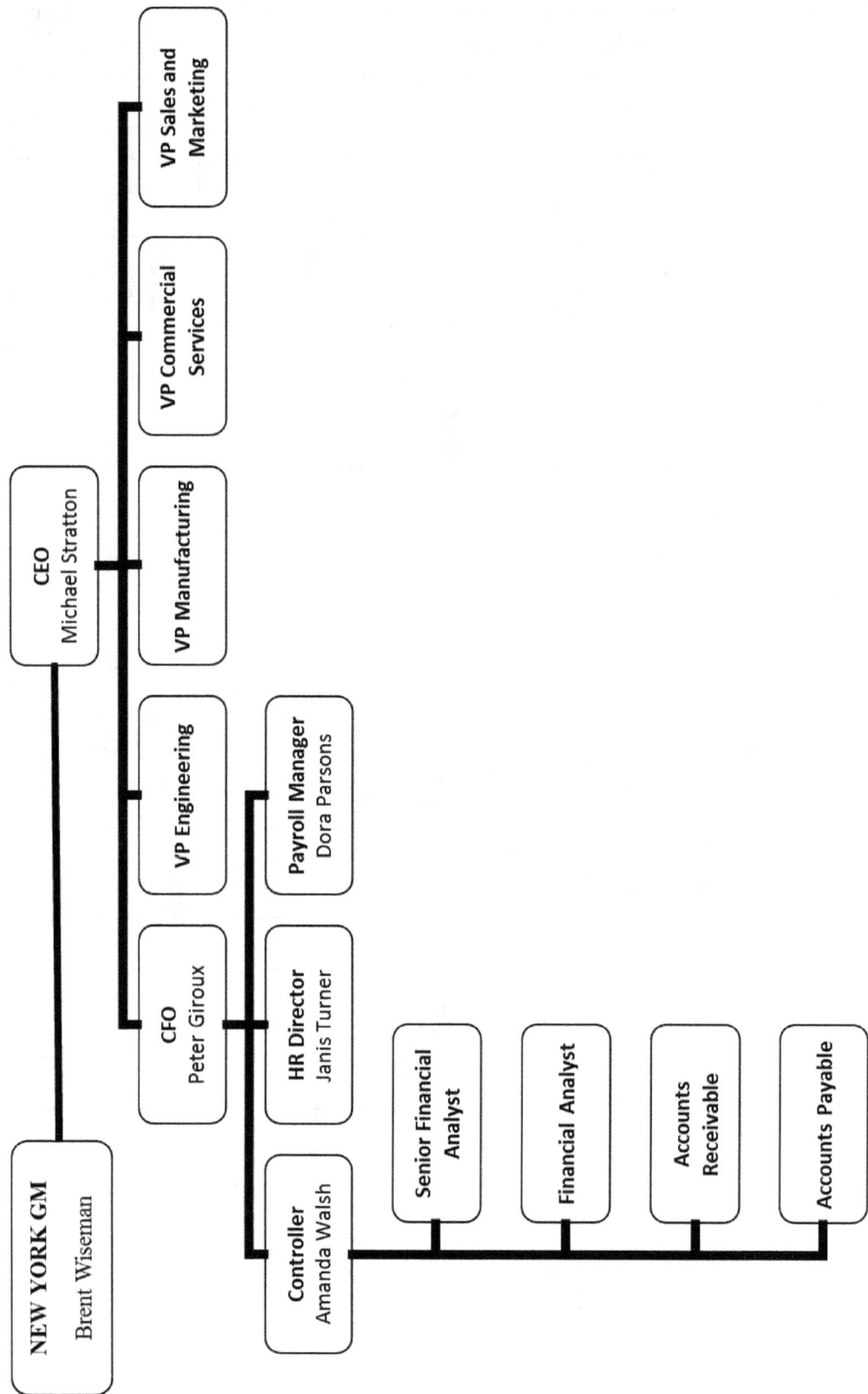

Exhibit 3: – Extract from Consolidated Financial Statements

Vanderville Plastics Company
Consolidated Balance Sheet
As of November 30

	2003 $	2002 $
Assets		
Current assets		
Cash	$ 469,402	$ 735,338
Accounts receivable	$ 5,193,806	$ 7,801,771
Inventories	$ 8,555,649	$ 9,270,595
Prepaid expenses and other current assets	$ 938,395	$ 878,962
Income taxes receivable	$ 2,200	$ -
	$ 15,159,452	$ 18,686,666
Property, equipment and improvements	$ 19,806,564	$ 21,530,031
Goodwill	$ -	$ 23,139,794
Deferred financing costs	$ 645,470	$ 936,977
Investments and other assets	$ 14,157	$ 13,153
	$ 35,625,643	$ 64,306,619
Liabilities		
Current liabilities		
Bank indebtedness	$ 6,535,659	$ 5,487,999
Accounts payable and accrued liabilities	$ 13,758,482	$ 11,996,282
Income taxes payable	$ -	$ 293,183
Customer deposits	$ 8,375,480	$ 10,937,110
Current portion of long-term debt	$ 28,316,006	$ 2,798,949
	$ 56,985,628	$ 31,513,523
Long-term debt	$ 2,084,833	$ 29,599,167
Loans payable	$ 6,540,233	$ 5,071,542
Deferred income taxes	$ 717,816	$ 487,787
	$ 66,328,510	$ 66,672,020
Contingencies and commitments		
Shareholders' Deficiency		
Capital stock	$ 10,936,681	$ 10,340,496
Share subscription loans	$ (720,390)	$ (706,946)
Deficit	$ (40,919,157)	$ (11,998,951)
	$ (30,702,867)	$ (2,365,400)
	$ 35,625,643	$ 64,306,619

FOR DISCUSSION WITH MANAGEMENT ONLY - SUBJECT TO AMENDMENT
NOT TO BE FURTHER COMMUNICATED

Vanderville Plastics Company
Consolidated Statement of Operations
For the year ended November 30

		2003		2002
		$		$
Net sales	$	52,581,273	$	52,057,383
Cost of sales - excluding depreciation	$	40,656,119	$	37,748,017
	$	11,925,154	$	14,309,367
Expenses				
Selling, general and administrative	$	7,352,520	$	6,317,988
Interest expense				
Long-term	$	4,160,721	$	3,636,623
Bank charges	$	96,430	$	386,158
Depreciation of property, equipment and improvements	$	3,273,068	$	3,474,448
Foreign exchange translation loss	$	1,313,581	$	120,986
Research and development	$	869,705	$	457,663
Amortization of deferred financing costs	$	428,572	$	491,510
Loss on sale of property, equipment and improvements	$	5,597	$	4,866
Amortization of other assets	$	-	$	1,164,351
Interest income	$	(15,652)	$	(17,161)
Cumulative effect of change in accounting principle	$	23,139,794	$	-
	$	40,626,336	$	16,037,431
Loss before income taxes	$	(28,701,182)	$	(1,728,065)
Provision for (recovery of) income taxes				
Current	$	(2,200)	$	(40,416)
Deferred	$	230,029	$	498,286
	$	227,829	$	457,870
Net loss for the year	$	(28,929,011)	$	(2,185,934)

FOR DISCUSSION WITH MANAGEMENT ONLY - SUBJECT TO AMENDMENT
NOT TO BE FURTHER COMMUNICATED

Exhibit 4: Extract from Non-Consolidated Financial Statements

Vanderville Plastics Company - Meadowbrook
Non-consolidated Income Statement
For the year ended November 30

		2005
		$
		(unaudited)
Net sales	$	51,624,004
Cost of goods sold	$	41,777,871
Gross Margin	$	9,846,133
Expenses		
Research and development	$	834,369
Selling and marketing	$	1,540,813
Administration	$	3,833,776
	$	6,208,958
EBITDA	$	3,637,176
Miami management fee	$	232,598
Owner driven consulting	$	657,768
Depreciation	$	2,787,321
Bank charges	$	28,956
Interest expense	$	4,539,446
Translation (gain)/loss	$	(581,977)
Interest income	$	(21,504)
	$	7,642,609
Loss before income taxes	$	(4,005,433)
Provision for (recovery of) income taxes		
Current	$	-
Deferred	$	-
	$	-
Net loss for the year	$	(4,005,433)
Prepared by Amanda Walsh, CMA		

Exhibit 5: EBITDA to Cash Reconciliation

Cash balance as of November 1st, 2005	$500,000
November working capital funding from Houston	$3,000,000
EBITDA for the quarter ended February 28, 2006	$900,000
Capital expenditures	($50,000)
Cash interest	($250,000)
Changes in working capital	($4,000,000)
Ending cash balance as of February 28th, 2006	$100,000

Prepared by Amanda Walsh, CMA

Notes

[1] CMA Canada granted the CMA designation in accounting through its provincial and territorial affiliated bodies until September 2015. The accounting profession was unified in Canada in 2014 under the umbrella of the Certified Professional Accountants of Canada (CPA Canada). Existing members retained their current professional designations but were also granted the new CPA designation. They are required to use the new CPA designation in conjunction with their existing designation for a period of 10 years. The Canadian CMA designation is different from the US CMA, a global designation granted by the Institute of Management Accountants.

[2] Financial statements prepared in accordance with generally accepted accounting principles (GAAP) in the US and internationally assume the reporting entity will continue as a going concern. According to Accounting Standards Update 2014-15, management should evaluate whether there are conditions or events that raise substantial doubt about the entity's ability to continue as a going concern within one year of the date the interim or annual financial statements are issued. When such conditions or events exist, the entity must disclose in a note to the financial statements information that enable users to understand these conditions and events, management's evaluation of their significance and its plans that are intended to mitigate these conditions or events (FASB, 2014).

[3] *Statement of Financial Accounting Standard (SFAS) 15 – Accounting by Debtors and Creditors for Troubled Debt Restructurings* defines a troubled debt restructuring as one in which the creditor grants a concession to the debtor that it would not otherwise consider, for economic or legal reasons (FASB, 1977). The debtor is allowed to reduce the carrying amount of the troubled debt to an amount equal to the total future cash payments specified by the new terms and recognize a gain on restructuring if the total future cash payments specified by the new terms are less than the carrying amount of the troubled debt (SFAS 15, paragraph 17).

[4] VPC used the completed-contract method to recognize revenues from its long-term manufacturing contracts. Consistent *with Accounting Research Bulletin (ARB) 45 – Long-Term Construction-Type Contracts*, manufacturing costs were deferred in work-in-process inventory until a contract was completed, with no revenue other than provision for expected losses being recorded until then. Estimates of costs to complete for each uncompleted contract were made at year-end to determine whether there were expected losses that needed to be provisioned.

Arkansas Egg Company:
Cracks in the Specialty Egg Market

NACRA
NORTH AMERICAN CASE
RESEARCH ASSOCIATION

David G. Hyatt, University of Arkansas

Michael Cox had a problem. As president of Arkansas Egg Company (AEC) based in rural Summers, Arkansas, he produced organic cage-free eggs for a living, but consumers were not buying them. It was early September of 2016 and the retail specialty egg market, which included cage-free, was weak, mostly due to an oversupply of conventional caged white eggs. Until now, the market for specialty eggs, reflecting consumer preferences for supporting small farmers, improved animal welfare, and organic food, had been growing steadily, but these eggs cost much more to produce and were more expensive in the store. As Cox described the relationship,

> A shift to sustainable farming practices (with a focus on animal welfare) is dependent on the consumers' willingness to pay more for that item and understand why it costs more. Organic farming has been a breath of life into small farms across the country. It creates an environment where the focus is on doing the right thing, not the cheapest thing. As a result the products cost more to produce and net more income that sustain this method of production.[1]

Conventional caged eggs were a commodity and producer prices were sensitive to shifts in supply and demand. But specialty eggs were often grown under contracts that protected producers, and the current oversupply meant that consumer prices of conventional eggs had plummeted, while specialty egg prices remained high. This differential had gotten so large that consumers of specialty eggs were switching back to conventional eggs. Cox could not remember a time when prices for on-shelf conventional caged-eggs had fallen so low that they affected consumer demand for specialty eggs. Cox bemoaned his situation:

> This is the first time that a bad caged market has affected the specialty market. You go to the grocery store and you see 75-cent white caged eggs, you're going to buy those eggs, not our $5 eggs. White eggs have gotten so cheap that it's pulling our consumer base away.[2]

Until now, his margins on production had been largely protected by a key contract with CCF Brands, a wholesaler of packaged foods, including organic eggs. But that

----

contract would expire on October 1, and Cox would be competing in the open market for egg prices that were now a fraction of his production costs. Cox wondered how he could protect his investment and minimize his losses.

THE ARKANSAS EGG COMPANY

Michael Cox was a third-generation egg producer. Over time, the family had built a vertically integrated company for conventional caged, white egg production, meaning that the operations included a feed mill, pullet houses for raising baby chicks, houses for hens to lay eggs, a production facility to clean, grade and pack eggs, and a refrigerated warehouse to store eggs for customer pickup. The operation peaked production with around 2.5 million hens, but his father closed the business in the 1990's during a sharp downturn in the egg market,

> My grandpa was with Cargill—that's who he retired with—but my dad was an independent cage producer in the '80s and '90s. The market really crashed, bad, in 1999 and that was kind of the end of that. It was just one of those cyclical bad crashes that the little guys have a hard time withstanding. So he was one of the larger independent producers in the country, but trying to sell independently in that market without sales locked up, you can't survive.

Cox purchased the assets from the business and created Arkansas Egg Company in 2001.

By 2007, aiming to differentiate his product, Cox began to shift from conventional caged-egg production to specialty eggs. Product marketing attributes in the specialty egg market affected the food or welfare of the hen laying the egg. This included organic feed, cage-free production, cage-free with outdoor access (free-range or pasture-raised), or other dimensions that commercial customers might demand.[3] Cox first contracted with Arkansas-based CCF Brands to produce organic, cage-free eggs for its Great Day Farms label, sold in Walmart stores.[4] The timing was good for Cox, who was concerned about poultry welfare issues and, just like his father before him, was hard-pressed to compete in the conventional market,

> We converted into organic production for several reasons. One, we had old, run down facilities which helped me see firsthand the environmental and welfare issues that accompanied conventional production. Second, the market for organic was stable compared to the conventional side. We could obtain the margins we needed to do a lot of things differently, the right way.[5]

Cox continued to expand operations in the specialty egg market. In 2010, AEC partnered with Texas-based Vital Farms, becoming first company in the nation to commercially produce pasture-raised eggs. Using contract growers, in 2012 AEC became Happy Egg Co.'s first U.S. producer and packer for its free-range certified brand.[6] Cox reflected on the value AEC provided to egg consumers and family farmers,

> My dad was a mass producer of cheap egg and he felt like his good work was providing the lowest cost product to the consumer. Now we have a lot of stakeholders, a lot of family farms. And we're creating a better life for a lot of different people on both ends. It does cost a little bit more, but the consumers that buy our eggs feel good that their purchase is directly impacting family farmers. Some companies want to be on the right side of change, and that is where are at.

By 2016, Cox was servicing these three contracts, as well as selling on the open market, with production from his own farms and from 25 contract growers in Arkansas and Missouri. His contract production in Missouri comprised 320,000 hens producing free-range eggs. His production on his own farms in Arkansas included 38,000 hens producing pasture-raised eggs and 130,000 hens that were producing organic cage-free eggs for the now expiring CCF Brands contract.

CCF Brands contracted for the output of a certain number of hens (up to 150,000) at a set price. Although Cox could profit by achieving higher-than-average egg production with efficient feed conversion, he also risked losses if production was below average. While his contracts contained feed escalator clauses that largely protected Cox from changes in feed costs, to achieve expected profit margins of 6-8 percent, Cox had to keep costs low and production high. Cox elaborated on his approach and the costs:

> We use the Hyline Brown breed—commercial layers that will lay 26 to 28 dozen eggs in their lifetime. They're good layers, are hardy, calm, and have good feed conversion. We get them from the hatchery at 95 cents, 35 to 80 thousand chicks at a time. By 24 weeks, when they really start laying, we've got $6.35 invested in cage-free and $10.64 in organic cage-free. Over their life, cage-free hens will cost us about $1.10 a dozen and organic cage-free hens will cost us about $1.70 a dozen. That $1.70 includes the original investment, feed, compliance, transportation and other direct costs, as well as 16 cents long-term debt and overhead.

On average, peak hen egg production occurred around week 31 and decreased thereafter. (Table 1 provides an approximation of the production pattern.) Generally Cox considered hens "productive" for 55 weeks beginning with week 24 and ending with week 78, when the hens were "spent." Hens were spent when they were not producing many eggs, but they were still consuming the same amount of food and thus it was no longer financially feasible to keep the hens alive and in production.

Table 1. Production patterns

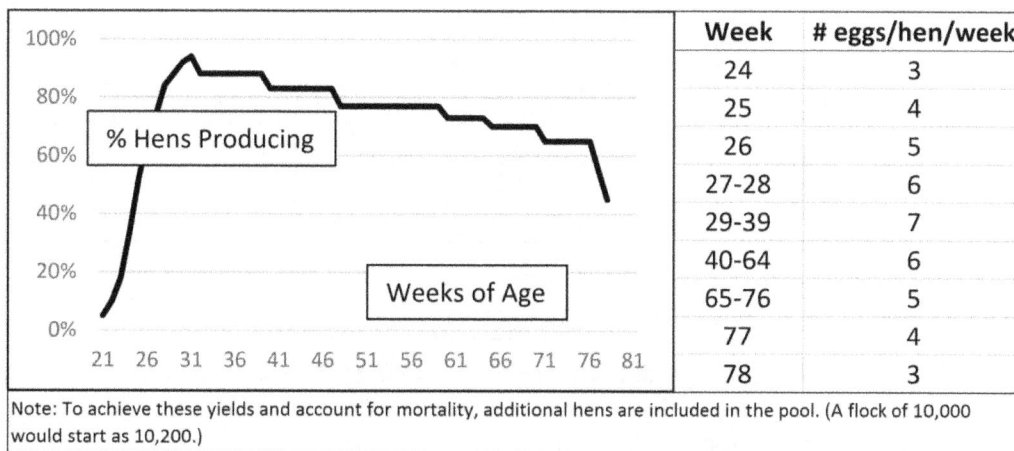

Week	# eggs/hen/week
24	3
25	4
26	5
27-28	6
29-39	7
40-64	6
65-76	5
77	4
78	3

Note: To achieve these yields and account for mortality, additional hens are included in the pool. (A flock of 10,000 would start as 10,200.)

Adapted from: Food and Agriculture Organization of the United Nations (FAO). 2010. *Egg Marketing: A Guide for the Production and Sale of Eggs*. http://teca.fao.org/read/6895.

When the hens were spent, the layer house was "depopulated," costing about 14–16 cents per hen, and the house was readied for the next flock.[7] Although AEC had previously explored various end-of-life alternatives, including specialty food markets and other products like salad toppings, pizza toppings, sausage, and even dog food, in

2016 there were no options for recovering any value from hens after 78 weeks. Cox described the situation, exacerbated by the fact that laying hens were a third of the size of hens raised for meat,

> What we run into is that these are old birds—this is an 80-week-old bird relative to a 35- to 50-day-old meat chicken you're getting from the store. The texture's different, the flavor profile's different, and it's not really something American consumers like. And from a cost standpoint, the yield of meat from a layer hen is minuscule compared to a meat bird, and considering the processing cost in a meat plant, you just can't justify it. At the end of the day you have a product that costs more per pound to create that visually looks worse and that tastes worse, to the American consumer.

At the two layer farms in Arkansas (called Summers and Thomas) servicing the organic cage-free eggs contract for CCF Brands, Cox was operating 12 layer houses with about 130,000 hens (see Table 2). The contract specified that CCF Brands would accept the output of up to 150,000 hens at a set price. Cox aimed to produce at least 26.6 dozen eggs per hen over its productive life. If he produced 26.6 dozen, he could operate with a normal profit margin and recover costs. If he produced more, he could achieve greater profit on the remaining eggs produced (having recovered his costs). If he produced less than 26.6 dozen, he could potentially lose money. Without the contract, Cox would have to sell eggs on the open market where brown eggs were trading at around 30 cents per dozen.[8] (See Exhibit 1 for additional cost and production information.)

Table 2. Arkansas Egg Company organic cage-free hen populations.

Hens (approximate)	Farm, barn number, and age of hens in barn
30,000	Summers #1 (15,000) & #5 (15,000): 48 weeks
15,000	Summers #2: 40 weeks
	Summers #3: Empty due to regular flock transition
15,000	Summers #4: 34 weeks
10,000	Thomas #21: 47 weeks
20,000	Thomas #22 (10,000) & #23 (10,000): 58 weeks
20,000	Thomas #24 (10,000) & #25 (10,000): 45 weeks
20,000	Thomas #26 (10,000) & #27 (10,000): 40 weeks
Note: Hen ages estimated as of the date of the contract expiration.	

EGG INDUSTRY MARKET DYNAMICS

In the United States, the $6.6 billon, mature shell-egg industry was dominated by large-scale, vertically-integrated producers of caged eggs. Sixty-four egg producers accounted for approximately 85% of the total production of 83 billion eggs from a domestic stock of about 302 million hens. About 88% of these hens supplied conventional eggs, and 12% produced specialty eggs, and most of the production supplied retailer and foodservice firms' demand.[9] Even given the current weak market for specialty eggs, Cox felt that it was poised to grow dramatically over the long term: More than 100 large-volume purchasers, including Walmart, McDonald's, Compass Foods, and Unilever, had recently committed to 100 percent cage-free eggs by 2025. This was projected to affect over 50% of egg production in the United States.

The egg market overall was cyclical and depended on multiple factors, including feed costs and the lead time required to bring hens into production. In addition, seasonal demand variation made life tough for producers. Cox described how demand changed over the year.

> The egg market is one of the most volatile commodity markets there is. Not only are there fluctuations with feed costs but there are significant demand changes over the year. Usually about the time school starts in August, demand hits. You've got cafeterias that are cooking eggs every morning and things like that. And then through the holidays, demand exceeds supply through Thanksgiving and Christmas, all the way to Easter. Then around May 1st, demand falls until school starts again.

However, the September 2016 market oversupply problem was related more to the ripple effects of an avian flu outbreak that began in the U.S. during December 2014 and continued through the middle of 2015. This outbreak had devastating effects on egg production; at least 35 million hens were lost by June 2015 from a base of nearly 310 million in January 2015.[10] That loss, and the subsequent restocking, had sent prices spiraling upward in 2015, then crashing down again in 2016.[11] (See Exhibit 2.) Cox described the dire impact of the situation on smaller producers and his optimism for a market rebound in the fall:

> This market fell off a cliff in early spring of 2016. The egg market usually goes through huge cycles, like seven-year cycles, but this is the worst that we've seen. By early spring of this year growers had their farms restocked, and basically the market flooded. A lot of small growers are going out of business. People hang on until they can't anymore. Part of what has me holding on is that historically the market turns around. So if you're looking at this in the summer you think, man, things stink now, but hey, the worse things are now, maybe the more likely they are to come back in the fall.

Complicating things for Cox, competition also was heating up because the largest producers in the industry moved into the specialty market in response to the cage-free commitments by the retailers and foodservice firms. These producers operated large, integrated complexes (often with more than a million hens) and took advantage of that scale to lower their costs. Because the cage-free standards (with the exception of organic) did not require access to the outdoors, high-volume producers could easily convert their facilities to achieve this standard. At the same time, as larger conventional producers made this shift, they would either have to cut production or expand facilities. Cage-free hens required at least double the space of conventional hens. How this shift happened would influence the supply of both conventional and specialty eggs. Already, the U.S. cage-free hen inventory had doubled from 6 percent of the total flock in April 2015 to 12 percent in August 2016.

MOVING FORWARD

Michael Cox considered what to do about the expiring contract with CCF Brands and the 130,000 hens supplying that contract. Future marginal cost from these birds would exceed marginal revenue. Although he had known far in advance that the contract would not be renewed, Cox had not been overly concerned because prices were good. But now, given the industry's current oversupply, it would be tough securing another contract with favorable terms.

Should he hang on through the current laying cycle, hoping for a market rebound in the fourth quarter? Market conditions usually improved in the fall and early winter as schools were in session and as holiday cooking required eggs. If market conditions improved, so would the possibility of contracts. Further, some of the largest food retail and foodservice companies were making commitments for procuring specialty eggs (cage-free). While these commitments were for the years 2020-2025, many large farms producing conventional eggs would need to cut production to meet the cage-free demand (barns that housed 10,000 hens in cages housed less than 5,000 cage-free). As supply of conventional eggs decreased, demand should be restored for Cox's organic eggs as the decreasing price differential drew consumers of organic eggs back.

Holding on would mean selling on the spot market through Egg Clearing House Incorporated, where brown eggs were trading at around 30 cents per dozen. White eggs were even cheaper.

He wondered if he should depopulate the flock; contractors would kill the hens humanely and dispose of them at the county landfill. That would probably also mean laying off the employees currently working in those houses. What if he got a contract opportunity, but had no chickens to fulfill it? He had to count on 6 months lead time to get back into production. Further, if he did depopulate, he gave up all possibility of recovering his initial investment. While depopulating hen houses was a fact of life for Cox, as a producer concerned with hen welfare, it was never easy to do.

Exhibit 1. Arkansas Egg Company Cost and Production Information

Arkansas Egg aimed to collect 26.6 dozen eggs from each hen over its productive laying cycle of 55 weeks. If that happened, based on the contract price, then AEC recovered the costs of bringing the bird to its productive cycle (about 40 cents/dozen) as well as fixed overhead (about 16 cents/dozen). The approximate contribution margin during this time was 7%. After the breakeven point, the only costs incurred were the variable production costs.

Information on hen life cycle	
Approximate life of hen	78 weeks
Pre-productive period of hen life cycle	First 23 weeks of life
Productive period or laying cycle	Last 55 weeks of life
Average age of laying hens at Summers' barns	43 weeks
Average age of laying hens at Thomas' barns	48 weeks
Minimum production target (PT) over which to allocate costs	26.6 dozen
Approximate costs based on 26.6 dozen production target	
Total pre-production cost through week 23	$0.40 per dozen or $10.64 per bird
Fixed overhead cost (facilities, debt service, depopulation, etc.)	$0.16 per dozen or $4.26 per bird
Variable production costs (feed, transportation, labor, etc.)	$1.14 per dozen or $30.32 per bird
Total cost for producing organic cage-free eggs	$1.70 per dozen or $45.22 per bird
Expected profit at 26.6 dozen (7%)	$0.12 per dozen or $3.17 per bird

Note: Arkansas Egg Company, as a family business with less than $25 million in revenue, used cash basis accounting for book and tax purposes. For purposes of this case, assume that revenue was produced after eggs are laid. Fixed and variable production costs were incurred evenly across the hen production cycle.

Exhibit 2. Trends in the Conventional Egg Market

	2016			2015				2014	
	Sep	Jun	Mar	Dec	Sep	Jun	Mar	Dec	Sep
Farm Price White Egg (doz.)	$ 0.40	$ 0.32	$ 0.67	$ 1.06	$ 1.70	$ 1.72	$ 1.24	$ 1.47	$ 0.85
Retail Price White Egg (doz.)[1]	$ 1.55	$ 1.49	$ 2.08	$ 2.75	$ 2.97	$ 2.57	$ 2.13	$ 2.21	$ 1.97
Table Egg Laying Hens (millions)[2]	307.6	301.0	302.4	286.6	275.6	269.9	304.1	307.8	302.1
	Q3	Q2	Q1	Q4	Q3	Q2	Q1	Q4	Q3
Table Egg Production (billions)[2]	22.4	21.6	21.1	20.2	19.5	20.3	21.5	22.2	21.6
Table Egg Demand (billions)[3]	20.2	21.4	21.4	20.8	19.7	20.0	20.9	21.9	21.4
Per Capita Demand (dozen eggs)[3]	69	66	66	64	61	62	65	68	67

[1] Source: Ibarburu, M., 2016 "U.S. egg cost of production and prices," Egg Industry Center.

[2] Source: USDA Economic Research Service. Livestock & Meat Domestic Data. Chickens and Eggs. Latest report available at: http://usda.mannlib.cornell.edu/MannUsda/viewDocumentInfo.do?documentID=1028

[3] Source: USDA Economic Research Service. World Agricultural Supply and Demand Estimates Report. Latest report available at: https://www.ers.usda.gov/data-products/livestock-meat-domestic-data/

Note: The USDA Cage-Free Shell Egg Report described that September prices to the first receiver (farm price) of organic cage-free eggs varied between $1.35 and $2.40. These were most likely contracted prices. Latest report available at https://www.ams.usda.gov/mnreports/pymcagefree.pdf

NOTES

[1] Vital Farms (July 21, 2011) "An Interview with Michael Cox, family farmer, Arkansas." Company website posting retrieved from https://vitalfarms.com/an-interview-with-michael-cox-family-farmer-arkansas/

[2] Unless otherwise noted, quotes from Michael Cox come from interviews conducted during September and October 2016.

[3] See this poster by the USDA that includes some information on egg marketing attributes: https://www.flickr.com/photos/usdagov/6904946814/sizes/o/

[4] See this link for information on CCF Brands operations: http://www.ccfbrands.com/great-day-farms.

[5] Vital Farms op. cit.

[6] See this link for information in Vital Farms: https://vitalfarms.com/ including an interview with Michael Cox here: https://vitalfarms.com/an-interview-with-michael-cox-family-farmer-arkansas/. Also, see this link for more about the Happy Egg Company: http://thehappyeggco.com/

[7] When Cox depopulated his houses, contractors normally came on site and euthanized the hens and removed them to the county landfill.

[8] In general, there is no difference between white and brown eggs. White chickens lay white eggs and red/brown chickens lay brown eggs. While the marketing attributes of organic, cage-free, etc. could be used in the production of either hen type, they were most often used with brown chickens. White chickens were smaller, ate less and were better suited to caged production environments. Cox means caged production when he says "white eggs."

[9] American Egg Board (2016) "About the U.S. Egg Industry." See also O'Keefe, Terrence (2015) "Top 21 U.S. egg company profiles," WATT Global Media; United Egg Producers (2016) "Egg Industry Fact Sheet."

[10] USDA (n.d.) HPAI 2014/15 Confirmed Detections; Ibarburu, M. (2016) "U.S. flock trends and projections," Egg Industry Center.

[11] Ibarburu, M. op. cit.

Murphy Stores: Capital Projects

NACRA
NORTH AMERICAN CASE
RESEARCH ASSOCIATION

John S. Strong, College of William and Mary

Tom Becker, Manager of Capital Planning for Murphy Stores, was reviewing possible projects that might be funded in 2007. The slowdown in the housing market had made Murphy's capital committee (which approved all capital spending over $1 million) cautious about a few investments that were aimed at increasing revenues; the capital committee now wanted to consider reallocating capital funds to cost-saving projects. Becker had previously been a project analyst, but had been promoted to Manager of Capital Planning (reporting to the Chief Financial Officer) not just for his technical financial skills, but also for his willingness to thoroughly discuss projects with members of the store operations and merchandising teams who were on the front lines of the business.

Murphy Stores was a large retailer with multiple brands and formats. There were large "full-line" department stores which carried a complete assortment of apparel, appliances, home goods, and general merchandise. (These stores were similar to Sears or JC Penney or Target.) The second format was smaller hardware stores which carried a moderate assortment of home improvement merchandise, comparable to larger Ace or True Value Hardware stores. The company also had small locally-franchised dealer stores, and tire and auto centers, but which were a much smaller part of the total business. Murphy had 200 full-line department stores and 200 hardware stores, with total revenues of about $10 billion.

Including online operations, the department store segment had experienced sales growth of about six percent annually for several years. Growth in home improvement spending had driven the hardware store sales growth at nine percent annually over the past five years. Murphy's total capital budget, like many broadline retailers, averaged about 1.5% - 2.0% of revenues, and about 4% - 7% of fixed assets. The 2007 capital budget had been revised downward from an initial $175 million to $150 million, as some projects were deferred. Historically, the company had allocated about 40 percent to reinvestment or replacement of existing assets, 35 percent to investments aimed at improving business operations and efficiency, and 25 percent to new growth initiatives. The company's weighted average cost of capital typically was applied for reinvestment or business improvement projects, with a varying premium of 2% to 4% for higher risk projects or growth initiatives.

The reallocation from revenue growth projects meant that Murphy Stores had approximately $7 million remaining in its capital budget for 2007. Becker was evaluating two potential cost-saving opportunities: enhanced security systems to reduce theft, and energy-efficient lighting replacements. Becker felt that considering these two potential investments would be well-received by the store operations managers. Becker commented, "Frequently, our operations team feels that the finance group doesn't really understand what is going on in stores." Becker felt that these two projects could help store managers deal with the growing amount of stolen merchandise and with the headache of continually having to change burned-out lighting and "dark spots" in departments.

Because both projects involved improvements to existing operations, Becker believed they could be analyzed using the standard weighted average cost of capital for the company. Becker noted,

> Our policy is to evaluate cost saving projects in existing stores on a consistent basis. We find it hard to estimate project specific discount rate adjustments. Instead, projects with less information should be subject to greater levels of sensitivity or scenario analysis. When we have undertaken *ex post* reviews, we have found more errors due to incorrect assumptions than any other factor.

Becker noted that the IRR calculations would help assess whether a higher discount rate would lead to a different project recommendation. Becker also commented that it was important not to double-count – that is, taking into account risk by changing variables in the cash flows as well as assuming higher discount rates.

The company's project evaluation review process assumed the company average tax rate of 39 percent and an average cost of capital of 12 percent, although this discount rate might be adjusted for projects of higher or lower risk. Each year, the capital planning team provided basic assumptions for capital project submissions, so that each division was not making its own determinations of general factors like inflation and the cost of capital. Becker also knew that the cost of capital could change, and had not been re-calculated recently, so he collected relevant financial market data to update his calculations. This data is presented in Exhibit 1 (next page). Being a fairly conservative organization, Murphy Stores had set its target capital structure with long-term debt at 20% of capital and equity at 80% of capital (measured at market values). The company typically used investment grade bond yields as its cost of debt, and believed that medium term Treasury notes and medium term spreads matched the asset lives of most of its investments.

Like many companies, however, Murphy's practice was to use a discount rate for its base case project evaluation slightly above the exact cost of capital as calculated, because the company felt this was a more conservative way to incorporate changes in financial markets and inherently optimistic project submissions. As one senior executive noted, "Nobody ever submits a project he doesn't like, so our base case analysis frequently turns out to be overly optimistic."

Becker knew that finance theory suggested that all positive NPV projects should be funded. However, in practice companies like Murphy Stores established capital budgets that operated within managerial constraints about the extent of external financing, required reinvestments, and the like. These constraints acted as a means of "soft" capital rationing, because any unfunded positive NPV projects were likely to be carried over and undertaken in the following year. Current revenue and expense forecasts indicated that there was no opportunity to increase the capital budget this year. Thus, it was only possible to recommend projects totaling $7 million.

Exhibit 1: Financial Market Data, 2007

Murphy Stores Equity Beta	1.20
Treasury bills (90 day)	4.00%
Medium term Treasury notes (10 years maturity)	4.50%
Long term Treasury bonds (30 year maturity)	5.00%
Corporate bonds Investment Grade (A)	6.75%
Corporate bonds Below Investment Grade (CCC)	10.50%
Prime Rate	7.25%
LIBOR (5 years)	5.80%
Expected Inflation	4%
Spreads (Rm - Rf)	
Rm-Rf (T-bills)	7.50%
Rm-Rf (T-notes)	7.00%
Rm-Rf (T-bonds)	6.50%
Rm-Rd (A rated corporate bonds)	4.75%
Return on S&P 500 (last 52 weeks)	14.60%

Sources: Morningstar, *SBBI Yearbook* 2007; *Standard and Poor's Bond Guide*; *The Wall Street Journal*; Value Line, 2007.

ELECTRONIC ARTICLE SURVEILLANCE (EAS)

EAS was a technology that utilized tags, entry and exit systems, and audible signals to deter merchandise theft. Many major retailers used EAS extensively. Increasingly, vendors were supplying products to stores with EAS source tags already attached. The most common version, and the one under consideration by Murphy, was the white sensor channels commonly seen just inside the exit doors of many stores. Radio Frequency Identification (RFID) chips were placed inside tags attached to merchandise using special devices that were required to remove them. If an attempt was made to remove a tagged item, a second RFID chip in the sensor channel sounded an alarm. Retail consulting studies indicated that stores that used EAS tended to drive shoplifters to stores without EAS. Other industry estimates suggested that shrink (industry terminology for stolen goods) fell 20% - 50% after EAS systems were installed.

Merchandise shrink was a hotly debated topic in the retail industry. Industry trade groups estimated that stolen merchandise (by customers, employees, suppliers, and system errors) equated to about 1.5% of total retail sales (and as high as 5%-7% in some sectors). There was much discussion and disagreement as to the source of shrink, but shoplifting by customers and by employees were believed to be much more significant than supplier theft or system reporting errors. Murphy believed that the presence of EAS would not only help reduce customer theft, but also deter employee theft because the tags had to be physically removed.

Current Murphy hardware store shrinkage in 2006 was about 3.1% of sales, up from 1.8% a year earlier. Full-line stores had shrink of 2.8% in 2006, compared with 1.8% in 2005. Full-line stores shrink by selected store departments are shown in Exhibit 2. Hardware store shrink had been growing steadily in recent years. Full-line store shrink had been more variable, but recent data indicated a sharp uptick to 3.6% in the first quarter of 2007.

Exhibit 2: Shrink as a Percentage of Sales by Category

Category	2006 Shrink	2005 Shrink
Full-line store, selected departments		
Computers	3.6%	2.1%
Home electronics	3.7%	2.4%
Womens Apparel	4.2%	3.8%
Mens Apparel	3.9%	2.5%
Average- full-line stores*	2.8%	1.8%
Average – hardware stores	3.1%	1.8%

Notes: Averages reported are across all departments, not just the four listed above. Full-line stores shrink in Q1 2007 3.6%)
Source: Company information.

Murphy's had installed EAS in three stores in high-risk markets in 2005. Store A subsequently experienced shrink of 1.3%, while Store B had a rate of 0.2%. Unfortunately, no pre-installation shrink data was available for these two stores. In Store C, shrink fell from 1.8% pre-EAS to 0.1% after the installation of EAS. Murphy's currently had EAS installed in 19 full-line stores and 5 hardware stores.

The proposed EAS initiative would install the systems in 23 full-line stores and/or 110 hardware stores in 2007. The initial costs for the full-line stores are shown in Exhibit 3. Ten years was the expected life of the project, with no salvage value. Of the total $4.6 million required, just over $3 million would be depreciated on a modified accelerated cost recovery system (MACRS) schedule, with the equipment classified in the seven year recovery period by the IRS. The MACRS seven year depreciation schedule is presented in Exhibit 4. The remainder would be expensed immediately. The only significant cash expense item going forward was the ongoing cost of tags, which needed to be replaced each year. It was assumed that labor costs to install and remove the tags would be taken care of by suppliers or existing sales staff during slow periods, so that there would be no incremental employee costs.

Similar cost estimates for the Hardware stores were shown in Exhibit 5. Again, the only significant expense going forward would be for label tags. However, because hardware stores included many items in which tags could be reused, only one-fourth of label tags would need to be replaced each year.

Exhibit 3: EAS Project Costs, Full-line Stores

Product/ Item	Cost per Store (thousands $)	Cost for Project (thousands $)	Category
Door Pedestal/Alarm	$ 41	$ 943	capital
Floor system	27	621	capital
Message Units	3	69	capital
Tags	68	1,564	expense
Installation	21	483	capital
Deactivator/Detachers	40	920	capital
Total capital	$ 132	$ 3,036	
Total expense	$ 68	$ 1,564	
Total cost	$ 200	$ 4,600	

Note: Capital category is subject to depreciation.
Source: Company information.

Exhibit 4: Modified Accelerated Depreciation Schedule (MACRS)
Seven Year Equipment Category

Year	Depreciation Rate %	Year	Depreciation Rate %
1	14.29%	5	8.93%
2	24.49%	6	8.92%
3	17.49%	7	8.93%
4	12.49%	8	4.46%

Note: Assumes half-year convention for the first year put in service; zero salvage value.

Exhibit 5: EAS Project Costs, Hardware Stores

Product/ Item	Cost per Store (thousands $)	Cost for Project (thousands $)	Category
Door Pedestal/Alarm	$ 10	$ 1,100	capital
Message Units	1	110	capital
Tags	2	220	expense
Installation	2	220	capital
Deactivator/Detachers	6	660	capital
Total capital	$ 19	$ 2,090	
Total expense	$ 2	$ 220	
Total cost	$ 21	$ 2,310	

Note: Capital category is subject to depreciation. No floor system is required in hardware stores because entry/exit is smaller and therefore can be contained in the door pedestal unit.
Source: Company information.

The financial benefit of reducing merchandise theft was also a topic of discussion. From a financial perspective, Becker felt that there were three possible ways to account for the benefit of reduced shrink:

1. Higher sales: Becker recalled that his finance classes in business school emphasized that sunk costs should not be considered in project evaluation. In the case of EAS, the cost of the merchandise was sunk, but the opportunity cost of the merchandise that was stolen was a lost sale. This would mean that the benefit of reducing shrink would be the higher differential sales that would result.

2. Cost savings: Becker also thought that it might be reasonable to assume that the cost to the company was replacing the merchandise that was stolen. Thus the benefit of reducing shrink would be the savings from not having to replenish merchandise – that is, the reduction in cost of goods sold. This meant that Murphy would not assume the replaced item would have been sold.

3. Higher gross margin dollars: Becker thought it would also be a good idea to discuss how the store operations and buying and merchandising teams thought about the benefits of reducing shrink from a managerial perspective. The retailers explained that stolen merchandise would have been sold. Their view was that shrink resulted in a lost sale, but as soon as an item was sold it would be replenished by the supplier. The supplier then included this estimated loss in the product cost paid by Murphy Stores. Murphy's executives thus believed the cost of shrink was the lost gross margin (differential margin = differential sales – differential cost of goods sold).

Becker decided that his analysis should take into account all of these approaches. If the EAS investments were attractive under all 3 approaches, this would likely strengthen support for implementation. If not, further discussion would be warranted. Because gross margin percentages were 44.7% for full-line stores and 40.8% for hardware stores, Becker realized that the calculated benefits from EAS would be higher for sales or cost of goods sold measures compared to the use of differential gross margin dollars. Becker thought it was ironic that the operations and merchandise team, who generally assumed optimistic forecasts, believed in a measure that would result in a lower estimate of financial benefits.

To undertake the analysis in full-line stores, Murphy's gross margin was 44.7%. Thus, each $1 of lost sales due to shrink represented 55.3 cents of cost of goods, and lost margin of 44.7 cents. If this shrink were reduced, there would be higher sales, lower costs, and higher gross margin dollars, each resulting in higher taxable income.

The systems would be installed in January, 2007, and benefits would begin midway through the year, so that the 2007 benefits would only be for six months. All cash flows were assumed to occur at the end of each year. Because the company did not have a lot of experience with EAS, Murphy's had decided to target its full-line store EAS investments on the categories shown in Exhibit 1. The total 2007 sales represented by these categories in the full-line stores were expected to be approximately $500 million (an average of $21.8 million in sales for each of the 23 full-line stores where EAS installation was being considered). Inflation was expected to average 4%; sales in full-line stores were expected to grow at 6% annually (including inflation).

For hardware stores, the affected 2007 sales were expected to be $406 million ($3.7 million times 110 stores). Sales were expected to grow at 9% annually (including the 4% inflation). Hardware store gross margins were 40.8%.

LIGHTING REPLACEMENT

The next potential project involved replacement of metal halide lighting fixtures with new generation fluorescent lighting (LED lighting was even more efficient, but was limited to more focused lighting, rather than general ceiling illumination of large store areas). The benefits of conversion were expected in three areas. First, the new lighting was much more energy-efficient and would reduce energy consumption 30%-40%. Second, the new lighting would create less heat and was thus expected to decrease air conditioning use. Third, the new lighting was expected to improve brightness and visibility by up to 75% compared with the old lights. Becker also felt that the new lighting technology would support the company's sustainability goals, although he felt it would be very hard to quantify these benefits.

The proposal would install this lighting in 187 hardware stores, at an average cost of $37,400 per store. Depreciation would be on a seven year MACRS basis. Ten years was the expected life of the project, with no salvage value. There would be negligible effects on bulb replacement rates and other ongoing investments relative to metal halide bulbs. Each store averaged 56.9 kilowatt-hours (kWh) of lighting-related electricity use per hour in 2006. Annual hours of store operation averaged 5,100, with an electricity cost of 7.5 cents per kWh. The lower heat levels produced by the new lighting were expected to reduce hourly electricity requirements for air conditioning in a typical store by 9-10 kilowatts. Air conditioning was typically in operation for 2,000 hours annually. The replacement would occur in early 2007, so again there would only be 6 months of savings in the first year.

RECCOMENDATION

Tom Becker knew his review would require building different financial models for EAS and for lighting. He felt that the uncertainty of assumptions would require him to pay careful attention to sensitivity and scenario analysis. Becker also realized that the projects were not necessarily mutually exclusive; it was possible to do some mix of EAS and lighting if the results warranted, as long as the total project investment did not exceed the $7 million of funds available. Becker felt that if the results were particularly attractive, any unfunded projects would receive high priority in the next budget cycle, which would start in only three months. Becker knew that Murphy's capital committee was awaiting his report. Because the capital committee was comprised of the CFO, controller, and heads of the operating units, Becker knew that they would have detailed questions and would expect him to be able to discuss project risks, sensitivities, and scenarios.

La Campaña de Marketing de Oilcorp: Reacciones Mixtas a una Iniciativa de Responsabilidad Social[1]

NACRA
NORTH AMERICAN CASE
RESEARCH ASSOCIATION

Juan Manuel Parra, Inalde Business School

En mayo de 2010, Carlos Cardona, de 35 años de edad y miembro del equipo de marketing de Oilcorp, estaba preocupado por las reacciones contradictorias que recibía una campaña social que la empresa estaba promoviendo en colaboración con la Cruz Roja. Algunos le cuestionaban abiertamente las motivaciones de la compañía, propietaria de la mayor cadena regional de estaciones de gasolina en Colombia, acusándola de utilizar una causa social para aumentar las ventas de combustible y persuadir a los clientes de dar sus datos personales para propósitos comerciales. Esto, para Carlos, significaba una alerta temprana.

Carlos revisó de nuevo el sitio web de la campaña y el plan de marketing. Cuando terminó, haciendo clic a lo largo de todo el proceso, una foto de un niño sonriente apareció en la última pantalla con un mensaje de "gracias". Un contador en el lateral de la pantalla mostró que poco más de 1.200 personas se habían inscrito en el sitio web. Carlos se percató de que, hasta la fecha, los resultados de la campaña estaban significativamente por debajo de las expectativas y que esto los alejaba de cumplir las promesas públicamente hechas por el CEO de Oilcorp. "¿Qué debemos hacer si no podemos satisfacer las proyecciones?" se preguntó Carlos.

OILCORP

Oilcorp era una empresa colombiana dedicada a la distribución y comercialización de combustibles y lubricantes, con fuerte presencia regional en el país (ver **Anexo 1**). Fue fundada en 1968 como una solución a la escasez de gasolina en la región noreste de Colombia. A lo largo del tiempo, se convirtió en una de las principales proveedoras de combustible para las regiones más remotas y más necesitadas, y reconocida como una firma preocupada por sus clientes. Para 2010, era una multinacional con presencia en seis países, la tercera empresa más grande de Colombia, y una de las de más rápido crecimiento en América Latina.

Oilcorp estaba muy orgullosa de sus valores (integridad, respeto, confianza, innovación y excelencia) y por su papel en la sociedad, tomando la Responsabilidad Social Corporativa (RSC)[2] muy en serio (ver **Anexos 2 y 3**). Realizaban trabajo social en todas las regiones donde operaba la empresa, con esfuerzos canalizados a través de la Fundación Oilcorp, centrándose en la educación y la cultura cívica.

Copyright © 2018 del *Case Research Journal* (CRJ) y de Juan Manuel Parra. Este caso fue preparado para discusión en clase, no para ilustrar la eficacia o ineficacia del manejo de situaciones administrativas. Las organizaciones, personas y eventos descritos en el caso son reales, pero han sido disfrazados con fines de confidencialidad. El autor desea agradecer a John J. Lawrence, Brent D. Beal, y los revisores anónimos del CRJ por sus útiles sugerencias sobre cómo hacer más eficaz este caso.

El Centenario de la Cruz Roja en Colombia

En enero de 2010, el Director de la Cruz Roja Colombiana presentó una propuesta al CEO de Oilcorp pidiendo ayuda para una iniciativa de recaudación de fondos. Como parte de la celebración de su centenario, la Cruz Roja quería sensibilizar al público sobre su labor y fomentar la periodicidad de las donaciones, por lo que estimaban que Oilcorp –debido a su reputación y presencia nacional- podría ayudarles a incrementar el reconocimiento de marca.

El CEO de Oilcorp remitió la propuesta a la División de Asuntos Corporativos (responsable de la Fundación Oilcorp, una organización que operaba de manera independiente), pero estos se negaron a participar porque no creían tener suficiente experiencia en estas actividades de marketing y el calendario propuesto era demasiado corto para realizar otra propuesta. Asimismo, ninguna actividad similar se había incluido en el presupuesto anual aprobado, por lo cual nadie en la Fundación estaba dispuesto a apropiarse de esta iniciativa. Como consecuencia, el proyecto fue delegado al Departamento de Marketing.

Los programas de responsabilidad corporativa y sostenibilidad de Oilcorp estaban principalmente orientados a promover la convivencia cívica y la promoción de la educación y la cultura ciudadana, en áreas donde las organizaciones sin fines de lucro (ONGs) no tenían una fuerte presencia. El equipo de marketing concluyó que la campaña tendría que hacer algo más que poner banderines y solicitar contribuciones de clientes en las estaciones de servicio o sugerir a los clientes que donaran su cambio en las compras de gasolina. Más aun, estos tipos de donaciones generarían problemas de logística y de control, pues Oilcorp tampoco era propietaria de todas las estaciones de servicio de su marca y al menos el 85% de sus estaciones estaban geográficamente dispersas por todo el país, muchas de ellas en zonas remotas. Así, sería casi imposible garantizar que las donaciones en efectivo depositadas en sus estaciones llegaran a la sede de la empresa.

Buscando una manera fácil de controlar y mantener los registros de donaciones, el equipo optó por dar una pequeña donación por galón vendido durante el mes de mayo. La donación sería efectuada directamente por Oilcorp (y no por las estaciones de servicio bajo licencia), por lo que saldría de su presupuesto anual, pero sin generar un impacto financiero significativo. La más exitosa de las estaciones de servicio en Bogotá, la ciudad más grande del país, vendía aproximadamente 150.000 galones mensuales, si bien el promedio mensual de ventas por estación en Bogotá era de 80.000 galones y cerca de 40.000 o 50.000 galones en el resto del país.

Al mismo tiempo, y dado que Oilcorp estaba intentando crear una comunidad de usuarios alrededor de la marca para promover la fidelización de clientes, el equipo de marketing decidió utilizar su propio sitio web para la campaña de recaudación de fondos. De esta forma, optaron por pedir información de los consumidores, dejando claro que –a cambio- Oilcorp daría una contribución adicional a la Cruz Roja Colombiana. Esto también permitiría a Oilcorp aprovechar los descuentos de publicidad para promover la campaña, por estar bajo marca compartida con una organización social como la Cruz Roja[3].

La Campaña "Llena Tu Coche de Felicidad"

Oilcorp diseñó una campaña publicitaria denominada "Llena tu coche de felicidad". Los clientes, cada uno de los 1.267 empleados Oilcorp (más otros 1.637 contratados a través de *outsourcing*), sumados a numerosos contactos en las bases de datos disponibles, recibieron un email pidiéndoles "llenar sus coches de felicidad… ¡más de una vez!". Los empleados mismos reenviaron el correo electrónico a sus contactos personales y cada estación de servicio distribuyó volantes con información.

El email decía que todo el mundo debería ayudar en la campaña por tratarse de una buena causa. Subrayaba que "donando unos pocos segundos de su tiempo, muchos niños tendrán la oportunidad de sonreír" e invitaba a los destinatarios del correo electrónico a enviarlo a su lista de contactos y "ayudar a construir un mañana mejor" siguiendo una serie de links.

La Cruz Roja también anunció la campaña a través de comunicados de prensa:

Cuando los colombianos se detienen en una de las más de 1.300 estaciones de servicio operadas por Oilcorp en todo el país, no sólo llenarán sus coches con combustible regular o premium , gasolina o diésel. También van a llenar sus vehículos de felicidad, ya que, por cada galón de combustible comprado, Oilcorp donará US$0,0005 (Col$1 peso) a la Cruz Roja Colombiana para apoyar su Programa de Atención Integrada a las Enfermedades Prevalentes de la Infancia y proveer atención médica a niños y mujeres embarazadas[4].

Uno de los enlaces mencionaba:

Otra forma en la cual todos los colombianos pueden contribuir a esta misión humanitaria es visitando nuestro sitio web, www.oilcorpworld.com. Por cada ciudadano que se registre, Oilcorp contribuirá una suma adicional de US$0,50 (Col$1.000 pesos) a la Cruz Roja.

En abril de 2010, la Cruz Roja Colombiana y Oilcorp lanzaron la campaña con spots de radio en algunas de las emisoras más populares. Los comunicados de prensa sugerían que la Cruz Roja Colombiana esperaba recaudar US$1.250 en ventas diarias de combustible durante el mes de mayo. Y el CEO de Oilcorp informó que, con las donaciones adicionales de los clientes que se estaban registrando en su sitio web, el total de la recaudación esperada era de US$50.000.[5]

UNA INCÓMODA COMPARACIÓN: LA PROMOCIÓN INSUPERABLE DE CHEVRONTEXACO

Cuando Carlos invitó a sus amigos a unirse a la campaña, le sorprendieron algunas sus reacciones. Quedó especialmente preocupado por los comentarios de Ricardo, un senior manager de 45 años de una gran multinacional con experiencia en *retail*. Especialmente porque, en opinión de Carlos, Ricardo tenía elevada sensibilidad ética y de responsabilidad social.

Ricardo era consciente de cuán frecuentemente organizaciones diversas le pedían ayuda a través de diferentes canales. Contribuía periódicamente parte del cambio recibido al comprar víveres en tiendas minoristas, y también hacía donaciones en campañas colocadas en cajeros automáticos y en las actividades de recaudación de fondos para obras benéficas de su empresa.

Unos meses antes, Ricardo había participado en una campaña ("La Promoción Insuperable") realizada por un importante competidor de Oilcorp (ChevronTexaco)[6]. La conoció después de visitar una de las estaciones de servicio cerca de su casa. Los clientes eran alentados a participar en un concurso para ganar premios, a cambio de registrarse en el sitio web, donde eran informados acerca de las principales características de un producto de ChevronTexaco (un tipo especial de gasolina, con un aditivo patentado y exclusivo llamado Techron). Ricardo nunca ganó nada, pero lo intentó en varias ocasiones. De hecho, la campaña seguía en curso después de varios ciclos y con diferentes premios[7].

Como parte de la promoción, ChevronTexaco contrató a Eccos Contact Center, una organización sin fines de lucro, cuyos objetivos incluían la capacitación de personas con discapacidad física que eran víctimas del conflicto armado colombiano (especialmente a las víctimas de las minas terrestres), promoviendo proyectos de vida viables y sostenibles destinados a desarrollar sus competencias cívicas y laborales. Esta información no era un secreto, pero no lo anunciaban.

La propia conciencia social de Ricardo estaba más desarrollada que lo normal. Estaba donando parte de su sueldo a una escuela en una zona deprimida en Bogotá, porque conocía el lugar y le parecía una situación dolorosa. La empresa para la que trabajaba tenía también una fundación dedicada a iniciativas sociales, aportando un ayuda importante pero discreta. Además, él participaba regularmente en campañas promovidas internamente entre el personal para ayudar a víctimas de inundaciones, o para comprar regalos de Navidad para niños enfermos. Sin embargo, Ricardo no se sintió igualmente atraído por la campaña de Oilcorp; por el contrario, le hizo sentir incómodo. No entendía por qué colocaban condiciones para "ayudar a los más necesitados " y por qué parecía que Oilcorp estaba aprovechándose de una causa social legítima para fines de marketing. Tampoco estaba seguro de por qué le estaban pidiendo registrarse en un sitio web a cambio de una donación que, pensaba, Oilcorp debía hacer por su propia cuenta.

El Dilema de Carlos: ¿Incentivos a la Generosidad?

A mediados de mayo, Carlos se reunió con el equipo de marketing para discutir las reacciones de sus amigos y abordar el hecho de que relativamente pocos individuos se habían registrado en el sitio web. Dijo al equipo que la reacción negativa más frecuente era: "si en realidad quieren ayudar, simplemente podrían dar dinero y no publicitarlo". También les informó que la campaña no estaba en vías de cumplir la meta del CEO de recaudar US$50.000 dólares para la Cruz Roja durante esta campaña, dado que solo tenía un mes de duración.

Durante la reunión, el Director de Publicidad se quejó de que la campaña con la Cruz Roja había sido una distracción. "¿No tenemos una alternativa más práctica para ayudarlos?", preguntó. "Nunca hemos hecho algo como esto". Pero el Vicepresidente de Marketing le respondió: "Recuerda lo que dijo nuestro CEO cuando supimos por primera vez de la iniciativa. No es un tema de marketing, sino de poner en práctica nuestros valores". Entretanto, el Director de la Fundación Oilcorp agregó: "Es importante porque quizás nuestra gran visibilidad es lo que ayude a movilizar estas causas comunes". Pero no estaba claro que la campaña estuviera logrando la meta de generar conciencia de marca, así como tampoco estaba claro que la participación Oilcorp estuviera motivando a sus clientes para contribuir.

"¿Qué plan de acción deberíamos adoptar a fin de cumplir con las expectativas de la Cruz Roja?" preguntó Carlos a su equipo.

ANEXO 1: Datos financieros de Oilcorp (al 31 de diciembre de 2009)

millones de dólares EE.UU.

Ingresos operacionales	$2.948,8
Beneficio neto	$97,3
Flujo de efectivo (al final del año)	$66,9
Total Activos	$1.241,8
Activos corrientes	$287,7
Total Pasivos	$504,7
Pasivos corrientes	$169,5

Fuente: Informe de Gestión Oilcorp 2009

ANEXO 2: Datos de la Fundación Oilcorp (a 31 de diciembre de 2009)

Total de ingresos procedentes de donaciones (en millones de US$)	$ 2.09
% de co-financiación de terceros	29,9%
% de recursos propios de Oilcorp	70,1%
# de personas beneficiadas:	194.000
Directamente	140.000
Indirectamente	54.000

Fuente: Informe de Gestión de la Fundación Oilcorp 2009

ANEXO 3: Algunos de los proyectos de Responsabilidad Social de Oilcorp

PROGRAMA	RESULTADOS
Global Reporting Initiative (GRI)	• Promovido por el CEO de Oilcorp para facilitar el aprendizaje organizacional sobre temas específicos (desarrollo de proveedores, creación de nuevas empresas de la mano de ex empleados, etc.). • Para la Bolsa de Valores de Colombia, el ejemplo de Oilcorp en esto era importante para estimular la transparencia y gobernabilidad
Programas para Stakeholders	• Accionistas y Gobierno Corporativo • Calidad de vida en el trabajo (con respecto a sus empleados) • Cuidado medioambiental de cara a la sociedad • Suministro responsable (con respecto a sus proveedores) • Desarrollo comunitario en áreas de influencia (programas adaptados a las circunstancias específicas de un país, y no un informe estándar determinado por casa matriz con intereses diferentes, como ayudar a niños abandonados en Ecuador o en el terremoto de 2010 en Chile) • Marketing responsable hacia los clientes
Comités de Inversión Social	• Operados a nivel regional • Objetivo de promover proyectos sociales en sus principales áreas de influencia a través del trabajo voluntario de sus empleados • Siete proyectos en 2008; casi 100 empleados en diferentes regiones aportando ideas, tiempo y know-how para 2.300 beneficiarios • Los proyectos incluyen: centro de estudios etnográficos; capacitación para hombres y mujeres cabezas de hogar (artesanías utilizando materiales reciclados, mecánica, artes y oficios, etc.); Centros Comunitarios con apoyo financiero de los empleados; Formación de niños y jóvenes como conciliadores de paz y mediadores de conflictos
Fundación Oilcorp	• Encaminada a desarrollar programas de educación cívica y cultural para mejorar conocimientos, valores y actitudes de ciudadanos y estudiantes, y promover un comportamiento responsable entre los conductores
Donaciones estratégicas	• Destinadas a varias fundaciones y proyectos regionales, a través de una política diseñada para priorizar la educación, la cultura, la recreación y la salud en áreas locales
Mercadeo responsable a los clientes	• Centrado en estudiar la completa satisfacción del cliente, los procedimientos de tramitación de quejas, y el seguimiento de los tiempos de entrega; promoción de cursos de capacitación para todos los involucrados en la cadena de valor de Oilcorp; I+D de nuevos productos que generen ahorros de combustible, permitiendo trayectos más largos y menos contaminación; y producción de gas natural para vehículos. Sitio web destinado a consumidores de las estaciones de servicio registrados en el programa, para que reciban boletines mensuales de la empresa y permanente asistencia en carretera.

NOTAS

[1] This case is the Spanish-language version of "Oilcorp's Marketing Campaign: Mixed Reactions to a CSR Initiative" which was originally published, in English, in the *Case Research Journal*, Volume 37, Issue 4.

[2] Valores Corporativos de Oilcorp: Integridad (comportarse con honestidad y coherencia); Respeto (construir relaciones internas justas, sólidas y transparentes, prestando atención a las necesidades de todos y manteniendo las promesas); Confianza (auto-regulación; creer en los demás, escuchar y valorar sus propuestas); Innovación (máxima exaltación de la orientación al cliente, a través de la diferenciación de propuestas y la inteligencia de mercado); y Excelencia (desarrollar a la organización y su gente).

[3] Los gastos de publicidad fueron estimados en aprox. US$120.000, incluyendo los descuentos ofrecidos por las estaciones de radio para la Cruz Roja. Un spot televisivo en prime time podría ser al menos 10 a 15 veces más costoso.

[4] El precio promedio mensual de un galón de gasolina regular en Colombia cambia según los precios del petróleo en el mercado mundial. En los tres meses antes, durante y después de la campaña de Oilcorp, los precios en Bogotá se movieron entre US$3,64 y US$3,73 por galón. Sin embargo, incluso si los precios de la gasolina están muy reglamentados en el mercado colombiano, el Gobierno ha permitido a cada estación fijar diferentes precios. Para conductores de taxis y camiones, una mínima diferencia de precios entre gasolineras puede representar un ahorro significativo. El margen libre para distribuidores (5,5%) no incluye los gastos de funcionamiento de las estaciones de servicio y tiene variaciones en diferentes zonas del país. El margen neto estimado por estación puede variar entre el 1,5% y el 4%. Un coche pequeño podría llenarse con aproximadamente 10 galones.

[5] US$1 = Col$2.000 pesos

[6] Chevron operaba una red nacional de casi 400 estaciones de servicio. Tenían 10-18% de cuota de mercado en combustible para automóviles y aviones, y en lubricantes. Bajo la marca de Texaco, desde 1958, la empresa vendía una línea completa de productos a través de estaciones, agentes de ventas y distribuidores en Colombia. La empresa también comercializaba lubricantes, refrigerantes y grasas bajo varias marcas de consumo, comercial e industrial. En 2007, Chevron comenzó a ofrecer combustibles que contenían el aditivo Techron®.

[7] De acuerdo con esta campaña, "cada vez que usted compra combustible en las estaciones de servicio Texaco identificadas con la promoción, recibirá una tarjeta con un código oculto de ocho letras. Usted recibirá una o más tarjetas, dependiendo de la cantidad de gasolina Texaco que ponga en su tanque". Los clientes tenían que introducir los códigos ocultos, bien a través de sus teléfonos celulares (por medio de mensajes de texto) o del sitio web. Algunos de los datos solicitados a los clientes incluían su región, información de contacto y tipo de vehículo. La lista de premios incluía 46 coches nuevos, televisores LCD de 90", 20 estéreos y 40 reproductores de DVD. El costo total de esos productos era de casi US$800.000 (suponiendo los precios de mercado). Texaco también asignó a esta promoción considerable pauta publicitaria en la mejor franja de televisión prime time durante los días laborables.